This book has been reviewed for accuracy by Patricia Romero, Towson State University

Published by Raintree Steck-Vaughn Publishers, an imprint of Steck-Vaughn Company

Italian text by Chiara Robertazzi
Illustrations for cover and interior by Giorgio Bacchin
English translation by Mary Di Ianni

Cover design by Cath Polito

Raintree Steck-Vaughn Art/Production

Joyce Spicer: Art Director

Electronic Production

Management by Design

English language typeset by Tom Fenton

Printed and bound in the United States of America

1 2 3 4 5 6 7 8 9 0   01 00 99 98 97 96

Library of Congress Cataloging-in-Publication Data
Robertazzi, Chiara.
   [Africa. English]
   Africa: (8th to 18th century) / by Chiara Robertazzi.
   p.   cm. — (History of the world)
   Includes index.
   Summary: Presents the many peoples, languages, cultures, religions, lifestyles, economies, wars, migrations, and political structures of Africa and how they provided the background for the rise and fall of civilizations of great power.
   ISBN 0-8172-4096-9
   1. Africa – History – Juvenile literature. [1. Africa – History.] I. Title. II. Series
   DT22.R63   1997   96-24636
   960 — dc20   CIP
                                                      AC

HISTORY OF THE WORLD

AFRICA
(8TH TO 18TH CENTURY)

RSVP

RAINTREE
STECK-VAUGHN
P U B L I S H E R S

The Steck-Vaughn Company

Austin, Texas

TABLE OF CONTENTS

Map labels:

Mediterranean Africa

Sahara Desert

Sub-Saharan Africa

Horn of Africa

Equatorial Forests

Great Lakes Area

ATLANTIC OCEAN

Madagascar

MAIN AFRICAN LINGUISTIC AREAS

Modern-day humans ("homo sapiens") represent one great species with many variations depending on racial mixture, migrations, and climatic and environmental differences. Using these differences to define race, as has been the case until recently, may be misleading. The concept of race has developed controversial undertones and usually ends with a superficial definition based on skin color. Particularly in Africa, the definition of race using this method is extremely problematic, given the many skin shades of its inhabitants. Today's scholars prefer to use language characteristics to distinguish and classify the various peoples. The most recent theories have classified the African peoples into five main linguistic groups: **1.** Afro-Asiatic languages; **2.** Nilo-Saharan languages; **3.** Niger-Congo languages; **4.** Khoisan languages; **5.** Malagasy dialects.

Legend:

Afro-Asiatic languages

Nilo-Saharan languages

Niger-Congo languages

Khoisan languages

Malagasy dialects

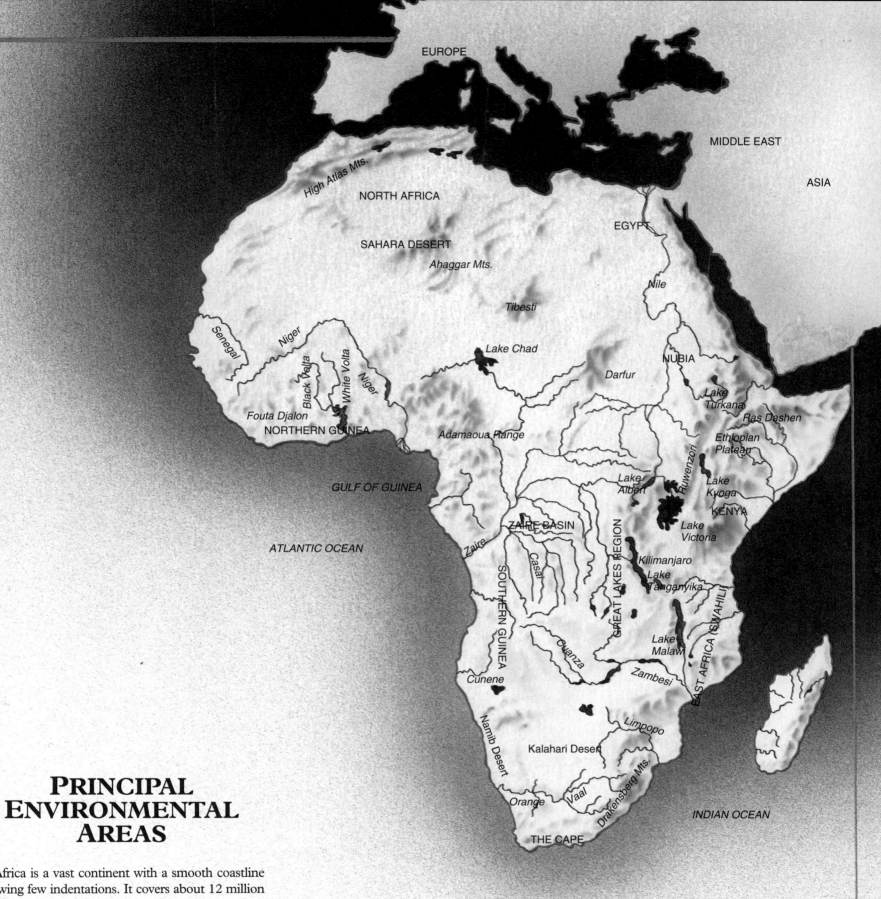

EUROPE

MIDDLE EAST

ASIA

High Atlas Mts.

NORTH AFRICA

SAHARA DESERT

EGYPT

Ahaggar Mts.

Nile

Tibesti

Senegal

Niger

Lake Chad

NUBIA

Black Volta

White Volta

Darfur

Lake
Turkana

Niger

Ras Dashen

Fouta Djalon

NORTHERN GUINEA

Adamaoua Range

Ethiopian
Plateau

Lake
Kyoga

GULF OF GUINEA

Lake
Albert

Ruwenzori

KENYA

ZAIRE BASIN

Lake
Victoria

ATLANTIC OCEAN

Zaire

Casai

GREAT LAKES REGION

Kilimanjaro
Lake
Tanganyika

SOUTHERN GUINEA

EAST AFRICA (SWAHILI)

Lake
Malawi

Cuanza

Namib Desert

Zambesi

Cunene

Limpopo

Kalahari Desert

Orange

Vaal

Drakensberg Mts.

INDIAN OCEAN

THE CAPE

PRINCIPAL ENVIRONMENTAL AREAS

Africa is a vast continent with a smooth coastline showing few indentations. It covers about 12 million square miles, is centered on the Equator, and extends over two hemispheres. The huge distances and apparent uniformity of African landscapes create an impression of vastness and monotony. Despite the relative continuity of the continent, we are able to distinguish each environment one after the other, starting from the Equator and moving north or south: equatorial rain forest gives way to the high grasses of the savanna; then comes the Sahel—semiarid bushland—followed by desert; and finally Mediterranean maquis, an area of dense growth of small trees and bushes.

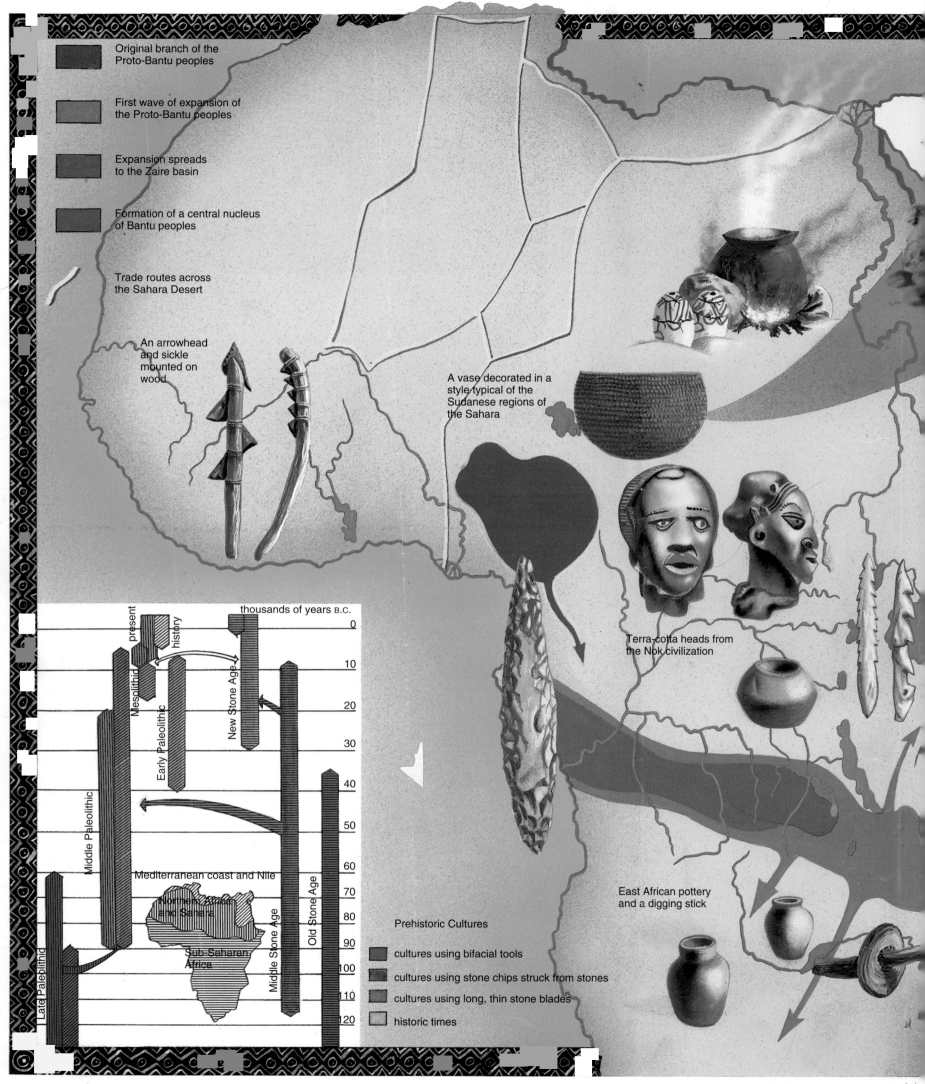

Original branch of the Proto-Bantu peoples

First wave of expansion of the Proto-Bantu peoples

Expansion spreads to the Zaire basin

Formation of a central nucleus of Bantu peoples

Trade routes across the Sahara Desert

An arrowhead and sickle mounted on wood

A vase decorated in a style typical of the Sudanese regions of the Sahara

Terra-cotta heads from the Nok civilization

East African pottery and a digging stick

thousands of years B.C.

present

history

Mesolithic

Early Paleolithic

New Stone Age

Middle Paleolithic

Mediterranean coast and Nile

Northern Africa and Sahara

Sub-Saharan Africa

Old Stone Age

Middle Stone Age

Late Paleolithic

0

10

20

30

40

50

60

70

80

90

100

110

120

Prehistoric Cultures

cultures using bifacial tools

cultures using stone chips struck from stones

cultures using long, thin stone blades

historic times

THE HISTORY OF AFRICAN CIVILIZATIONS

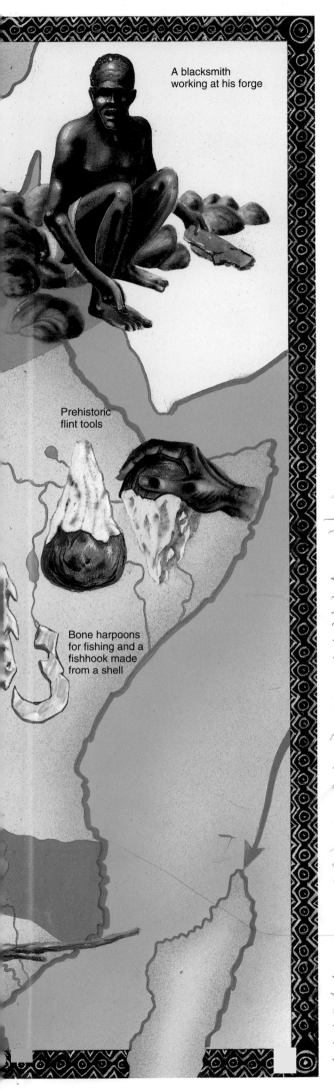

A blacksmith working at his forge

Prehistoric flint tools

Bone harpoons for fishing and a fishhook made from a shell

Like the story of humanity, the continuing story of African civilization is a constant reminder of humankind's basic ability to adapt to the environment and its cleverness in inventing the tools necessary to satisfy its needs.

The graph on page 6 shows the prehistoric stages of African history, from the Stone Age to the Iron Age. The vast majority of African civilizations had reached the end of the Iron Age by the 7th century, which is the beginning of the period examined in this book. The graph does not cover the great Egyptian, Phoenician, Roman, or Byzantine civilizations so important to the beginnings of African history in the Nile Valley and the Mediterranean coastal region. It is important, however, to remember the vast contributions those civilizations made to African history.

African history is full of fascinating events and details that have been widely recognized only in recent decades. Mysteries remain, and only further research and study will be able to clarify them.

The history of Africa is a vast subject, just as the continent itself is vast, populated by a wide range of complex societies. One glance at any map shows us that among all the continents, Africa is the most "compact" and the least influenced by the oceans surrounding it. Until the 15th century, the Atlantic coast was quite inaccessible to shipping because of the strong trade winds. These winds limited naval exploration by preventing the sailing ships from returning quickly to their home ports. On the other side of the continent, the coastal region facing the Indian Ocean has had contact with other areas on the Indian Ocean since before the birth of Christ. Inland from the coast is a dry, inhospitable area forming at least a partial barrier to communications. With the exception of the Mediterranean coastal region, Africa developed its own history in relative isolation. Nevertheless, contact between North Africa and what is today the area south of the Sahara Desert is known to have existed for many centuries. Until about 4000 B.C. the desert did not exist as a barrier to communication. And even after the climate became drier and the desert began to spread, people traveled back and forth on oxen, horses, and donkeys. Later, by the 2nd century A.D., the camel was introduced. Camels were able to carry between 50 and 60 pounds of goods and could go for a long time without water or food, making it possible for traders to move across the Sahara despite its expansion. South of the Sahara there are vast tropical areas and immense regions of desert, rain forests, huge lakes, and mountain chains.

Regional Variations

Historically African civilization was narrowly linked to two basic factors—the climatic conditions of each region, and their effects on food production, and the existence of natural obstacles in the landscape which interfered with communications between the members of different human settlements. Both factors explain the huge number and variety of peoples present on the continent together with their cultural and language differences. The problems of climate, food production, and communications also explain why some civilizations developed at different rates than others.

Already at the time of the ancient Egyptians, who created one of the world's greatest early civilizations, sub-Saharan Africa was the scene of slow evolution from the Paleolithic and Mesolithic Ages. During this time, certain regions showed a widespread distribution of the production and use of metals. This was so much the case that many regions of Africa are not considered to have experienced a Bronze Age, but to have passed from the Stone Age directly to the Iron Age, generally between 500 B.C. and A.D. 500 Throughout this long period, the cultural and historical divisions that characterized African evolution over the centuries began to take shape. In a certain way, these same variations still exist today.

Medieval Africa

Perhaps the expression "Medieval Africa" is not really the correct one to identify the period between the 7th and 17th centuries we are going to examine in this book. We use it just to make a time link with what was happening in European and world history during that period. "Medieval Africa" is rather misleading also because for several regions, West Africa in particular, this was the most important and in some ways the most splendid period in African history.

Let us begin by indicating the three basic features of African history during the Middle Ages. **1.** The spread of Islam, which established itself from the 7th century on, along the Mediterranean region of North Africa, the Sudanese regions, and in West Africa as a whole. It is important to emphasize that the influence of Islam was cultural and economic but was not characterized by direct political dominance at this time. It is also interesting to note that along the coasts of the Red Sea and the Indian Ocean, the influence of Islam often extended to political institutions. **2.** The completion of the Bantu migrations already begun in the first centuries A.D. The Bantu are a large subgroup of the Niger-Congo language group. The first Bantu speakers are thought to have originated somewhere on the border between present-day Cameroon and Nigeria. Because they were the parents of all Bantu speakers, their language is referred to as proto-Bantu. Try to think of languages as a tree. The root in this case is Niger-Congo, the trunk is proto-Bantu, and the branches are branches of Bantu that have spread across the central African continent. **3.** The arrival of European ships looking for alternative routes for the spice trade. They introduced the African coasts into the worldwide trading system that had Europe as its center. This upset the previous order, the extreme consequences of which would be revealed in the Atlantic slave trade.

Before examining these aspects more closely we want to pay attention to an important and typical feature influencing African history—the amazing variety and uniqueness of its origins. This discussion will follow in the next few pages.

GEOGRAPHICAL REGIONS AND ORIGINS OF AFRICAN HISTORY

Tassili rock paintings

Small brass sculpture of a drummer from the Hemba people of Zaire

AFRICA

Sahara Desert

Sub-Saharan Africa

The different climatic regions of Africa had an inevitable influence on the development of its agriculture and civilization. Such strongly contrasting regions as the desert, the savanna, the rain forests, the flat Atlantic coast with its lack of natural ports, and the coastal areas of the Indian Ocean so well suited to heavy maritime traffic, could never have developed in similar ways.

These contrasts made communications between the different communities extremely difficult. But they also created one of the fundamental aspects in the development of African civilization—the search to overcome the natural obstacles and find communication routes. This search is the basic foundation of the history of the African peoples.

To help describe the basic historical tendencies from the 7th to the 17th centuries, we have divided the continent into five principal regions: **1.** The Mediterranean coastal strip and the Nile Valley, up to the first cataract. This region was politically influenced by Muslim and Arab culture. The events dominating this region were historically both African and Muslim, but for reasons of limited space, here we shall only deal with the way these events influenced other African regions.

2. The Sahara Desert and the strip of savanna to the south—the Sudan. The two regions were closely linked during the period we shall examine, given that communications across the "sea of sand" had opened up because of the camel caravans. The peoples from the north and south had close contacts which alternated between trade and conquest.

3. Nubia and Ethiopia, centers of Christian resistance against the spread of Islam in North Africa.

4. The African coasts and the islands of the Indian Ocean, centers of a rich and complex maritime traffic with Asia, India, and Indonesia in particular.

5. South Africa. Because only limited information is available regarding the period we wish to study,

Sources of African History

Sources written in Arabic
Sources written in other languages (non-Arabic)
Oral tradition

Archeology
Linguistics
Anthropology
Ethnology
Ethnobotany
Figurative arts

A craftsman from the Kuba people (Zaire) making a drum. His tools, axes, and gouges are shown to the right of him.

Areas of Africa showing typical crafts: Tassali cave paintings from North Africa; wooden tablets bearing inscriptions from the Koran (from Central Sudan); pile-dwellings from the lake and river regions; a drummer sculpture from Zaire; and a craftsman making a drum, tools by his side.

Mediterranean Sea

Mediterranean Coast of Africa

ARABIA

Nile Valley

NUBIA

Twenty-inch-high wooden Haoussa tablet bearing Arabic inscriptions from the Koran, of the type often used in Muslim schools.

ETHIOPIA

A typical pile-dwelling made by people living in river or lake regions. This particular drawing shows a dwelling from the lakeside village of Ganvie in Benin.

SOUTH AFRICA

MADAGASCAR

we shall make suggestions that may have to wait for confirmation at a later date. What we do know about this region is that at this time the Bantu peoples continued their expansion and the Khoisan peoples gradually disappeared. Only small, isolated groups now remain, deep in the forest (the Pygmies), or in the far southwest (the Khoi-Khoi). We will examine details of particular interest regarding the kingdom of the Congo on the Atlantic coast and the region of Zimbabwe Monomotapa on the eastern side of the continent.

One of the basic problems facing researchers in compiling Africa's history is the lack of written sources. One way we have learned about African history is through the study of languages such as the proto-Bantu tree that produced the various branches of the language through migrations over time. For the early kingdoms south of the Sahara, we have to rely on writers who base much of their material on travelers' accounts.

For the historical period dealt with in this book, we draw on Al Masudi of Baghdad (10th century), Al Bakry of Spain (11th century), the Moroccan Al Idrisi (12th century), and Leo Africanus, in the Papal Court of Rome (16th century). All of these men based their writings on what they heard about the areas they describe. Ibn Battuta, another Moroccan, actually traveled widely in both West and East Africa in the 14th century. From the 15th century on we have the records of voyages and expeditions undertaken by European sailors and merchants. Certainly these are all "outside" sources, but cannot be neglected. The only real African source is the oral tradition, as can be seen from the list on page 8.

However, there are sources other than written accounts that can help us paint a clearer picture of the history of African civilization. Archeological digs have provided important evidence. Ethnology helps our understanding of the different cultures. Linguistics has helped to classify the different peoples. Ethnobotany reveals the earliest evidence about communication between the various peoples by studying the food crops produced in each region. Finally, but not least important, studying music and the visual arts reveals the values and beliefs that characterized African civilization in the past. The reconstruction of African history is therefore the combination of information gathered from a wide variety of sources. It has to include a large number of hypotheses which may be confirmed, amplified, denied, or substituted by further progress in research done in all these academic disciplines.

Instrument used by the griots perhaps for medical purposes, made from the skull of an African crow. It is attached to a gourd containing special ingredients believed to have magical powers.

A contemporary musician in Uganda

Handpainted Senufo cloth from the Ivory Coast, showing wild animals and some kind of firearm or fireworks

A scene from everyday village life in the Nigerian savanna region: woman pounding millet

THE ORAL TRADITION

The oral tradition, among all the sources regarding African history and geography, is especially important for what it can teach us about the Sudanese empires from the 10th to the 16th centuries, as well as what it can tell us about the rest of the continent. The oral tradition was a way to conserve and transmit the conscience and awareness of an entire people. Every aspect of community life is present: religious beliefs, dance, medicine, magic, war, relationship with the wise man, and moments of everyday life. The illustrations on pages 10–11 show various aspects connected with the oral tradition and its main themes: a typical scene from a north Nigerian village (women pounding millet); a piece of cloth where the symbol for the source of life appears several times; an instrument used by the oral historians, or "griots," for performing magic; a bag of objects also believed to have magical power; a Dogon statue of a dancer; the praying hands of a wise man, symbol of his communion with the spiritual world.

Except for the Egyptians, the Coptic Christians of Ethiopia, and the Islamic states of North Africa, the African peoples generally had no national form of writing. Many did, however, record their history through oral traditions. Some societies had a special caste, or class, whose members memorized and then recited the great feats of their society's leaders or important events in its past. These people were called griots. Use of that term has been extended to other societies where, for instance, certain people were chosen to keep a list of kings. In smaller societies, where law was made and interpreted by elders, the emphasis was usually on customs of the individual community. It was common for the elders to seek precedent as communicated through oral history.

Until very recently the oral tradition was not accepted as a valid historical source. It was regarded as unreliable, and often manipulated for their own purposes by specific interests both past and present. This attitude has changed over the last three decades. Researchers have realized that much information otherwise not available could be supplied by the oral tradition. Where cross-checking with written documents was possible, the information gathered from the oral tradition was often proved reliable. Moreover, even when cross-checking with information written in later Arab or European sources or found in archeological digs was impossible, historians realized that the stories passed down through the oral tradition were in themselves extremely important products of the ancient African civilizations. Those studying the history of Africa began to collect and translate sources of the oral tradition. This was a complicated and urgent task, especially because the conditions of modern life in Africa make it increasingly difficult for the older generations to pass the oral tradition down to the young. Translating and interpreting the oral tradition are also becoming more problematic.

The Griots of the Mande Cultures

Among the Mande speakers, who are also of the Niger-Congo language group, the past was considered very important. They took great care in passing their traditions on to each generation. The Mande founded the great empires of the western Sudan. The role of the Mande griots was to collect and transmit all the information about the grandeur and values of the founders of the kingdom and of the monarchs who followed them. They were a kind of professional "collector of memories." They represented a sort of storage place for civic and religious history; they were the custodians of their peoples' traditions. The griots received memory training from their early childhood, and the best among them accumulated an amazing body of knowledge. They were at the same time historians, musicians, poets, and philosophers. They even held important positions in the king's court. This is the way they defined themselves, a definition which has been passed down to us today: "We are sacks full of words, sacks holding the secrets of many centuries. The art of speech holds no secrets for us. Without us the king's name would be forgotten, we are the memory of men. Our words give life to the king's deeds for new generations. History has no mysteries for us."

Griots were also musicians and dancers. Among the Mande music and dance were very closely connected. There were a variety of musical instruments ranging from various sizes of drum, which accompanied each dance, to the "tubule," generally used in more exceptional situations such as the death or proclamation of a monarch, a war, or a fire. They also had tambourines and string instruments like the "nkoni," a three-stringed guitar, and wind instruments such as the flute, trumpets, and horns. The dancers wore amazing headdresses and masks which usually represented animals of the savanna. Their songs and chants spoke of everyday activities and the people's beliefs. They accompanied initiation ceremonies, hunting expeditions, and the rites particular to each ethnic group. Each social group had its own special songs and dances.

Fetish from the Baluba people of the Congo. The bag holds objects believed to be magic, used by medicine men and made of various organic and inorganic substances.

An elegant Dogon sculpture in iron. It shows a dancer; the objects hanging from its arms, foot, and head resemble castanets.

Two praying hands, those of an old man, which represent wisdom and a link with the spiritual world

THE SAHARA DESERT: LINK BETWEEN NORTH AND SOUTH

The Sahara Desert covers a quarter of the African continent. It has always played a basic role in African history and has separated Mediterranean Africa from sub-Saharan Africa since the time it became a total desert, around 2500 or 2000 B.C.. But it was also an area where the peoples living around it could meet and contact each other, like a vast internal sea linking the Mediterranean coastal strip with the areas to its immediate south. In ancient times the Romans and Byzantines had no specific name for the region. They simply called it the "unknown land," an uninhabitable place. It became a "link" only after the religion of Islam spread to the Mediterranean coastal strip and into Egypt. The Arabs called this region Sahara, meaning empty.

The desert is neither uniform nor monotonous— it is unexpectedly varied. There are areas of fine, gently waving sand—and there also are regions of small, round mounds of sand. At slightly higher elevations, there are the ever-changing landscapes of dunes and rock-strewn plateaus. In contrast, the lush oases offer shelter to caravans of people and camels and act as centers for the important livestock markets.

Between the desert and the tropical forest we find the region called the savanna. This is the Sudan—a vast area of prairie, with long grass, bushes, and a few isolated trees. The Sudan is a name of Arab origin, meaning "land of the black men" (the equivalent of "Ethiopia" for the ancient Greeks). In the past it referred to the whole strip of territory immediately to the south of the Sahara, while today it is only the name of one nation.

It is important to remember that before 2500–2000 B.C., the Sahara experienced a period of humidity. It was inhabited by large populations who left limited but significant evidence of their existence. The process of desertification probably began between 6000 and 5000 B.C. This process obviously destroyed the conditions that had supported human life. It also made the Sahara a barrier between the Mediterranean coastal strip and the rest of the continent, which even today is often called sub-Saharan Africa. It was never a totally impenetrable barrier. Contacts were maintained, above all by the nomad peoples of the desert such as the Berber shepherds, the famous Garamantes of Fezzan, in the central Sahara area south of Tripoli. They were mentioned by the Greek historian Herodotus, who described their use of four-wheeled carts to attack the "Ethio-pians"—the black-skinned men. The present-day Tuaregs are their descendants. Their society is organized according to strict ranks or classes, with rigid caste distinctions between nobles, subjects, and slaves. The Tuareg are known for the blue veil they wear, which partially covers the face. This custom probably arose as a way of keeping out the sand and dust.

For centuries the most important—and in many ways the only—route between the north and the south of the continent was the Nile Valley. During the 7th century A.D., the spread of Islam across all of North Africa began. This brought increased Islamic influence over the economy and culture of all regions of the Sudan. At this time the Sahara became an area of communications and exchanges once more. It was like a vast ocean crossed by the camel caravans. Camels had been introduced as an excellent form of desert transportation around the beginning of the Christian era. They only became more widely used during the 4th and 5th centuries, however, when the caravan traffic across the desert really flourished. In this way all of the Sudan region became included in the Islamic world in a certain sense.

The shading on the map shows the approximate areas of the Sahara and the Sudanese empires. Their importance and practically their whole existence depended on the desert. The camel caravans carried gold, slaves, and ivory to the north and salt—found abundantly in the Sahara—to the south, where there is very little. At the start of the period we will study, most of the desert traffic used the route between Morocco and the Empire of Ghana. Later the rise of the Mali Empire and afterward that of the Songhai caused the political and economic centers of the Sudan to move farther east. This was probably because of the rapid decline of the Almoravid and Almohad empires in the Morocco region. The remaining part of North Africa was increasingly dominated by the Hafsidi of Tunis during this period. In future chapters we shall take a closer look at the development of the west Sudanese empires together with that of the Kanem Empire in central Sudan.

Berber woman in traditional dress. The silver bracelet is the sign of passage into adulthood.

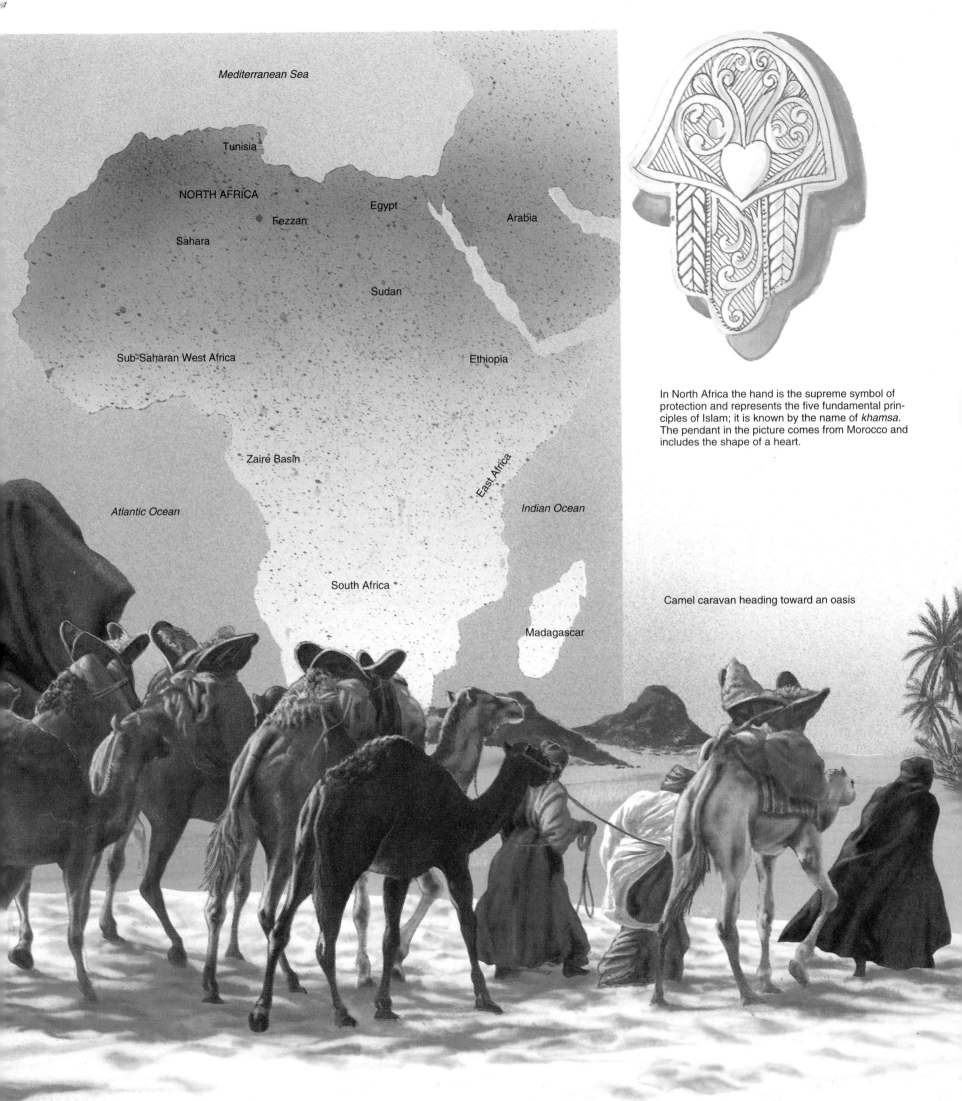

Mediterranean Sea

Tunisia

NORTH AFRICA

Fezzan

Egypt

Arabia

Sahara

Sudan

Sub-Saharan West Africa

Ethiopia

Zaire Basin

East Africa

Atlantic Ocean

Indian Ocean

South Africa

Madagascar

In North Africa the hand is the supreme symbol of protection and represents the five fundamental principles of Islam; it is known by the name of *khamsa*. The pendant in the picture comes from Morocco and includes the shape of a heart.

Camel caravan heading toward an oasis

13

THE BANTU-SPEAKING PEOPLES AND THEIR EXPANSION

Tutsi queen mother wearing traditional headdress to hide her face from strangers

Tanzanian woman

The term Bantu was introduced during the 19th century by an English linguistics (languages) scholar. It was intended to show the link between a series of languages spoken in much of sub-Saharan Africa. These linguistic ties were quite loose, however, given that over 350 Bantu languages existed in the region. Many peoples living in the area did not understand Bantu languages other than their own even though they were closely related. It is a mistake to suppose there is always a connection between language, ethnic group, and culture. Research has proved that many mixtures of the three exist. We should not be surprised to find that many anthropological differences exist between the various ethnic groups present in the region where Bantu languages are spoken. An excellent example can be seen with the two peoples of Rwanda, the Tutsi and Hutu.

Today the Bantu people occupy a large area in central and southern Africa, extending as far north as the Zaire (formerly Congo) River, and as far south as South Africa (except in the southwestern area inhabited by the Khoisan peoples). The Bantu area stretches eastward from the coast of West Africa to the Indian Ocean in the south (in the area of today's Mozambique), and to the area of Lake Victoria farther north. In Kenya, the Bantu are interspersed with the Nilo-Saharan peoples. The Bantu movements spanned centuries, and may be the most important migration in African history.

We know little about Bantu culture or history from the 5th to 8th centuries, but between the 8th and the 12th the majority of Bantu were farmers and livestock keepers. Some of them, however, continued as hunters and gatherers, while others mas-

The picture-map above on pages 14–15 shows a bird's eye view of the west coast of Africa. Typical representatives of different Bantu-speaking peoples are illustrated above the map to demonstrate their contrasting ethnic characteristics.

Mouth of Niger River

Afro-Asian language zone

Bantu language zone

Principal Bantu Language Groups

Languages of the Bantu group have derived from proto-Bantu and are generally located in the following areas:

Congo - Zaire and Congo
Miji Kenda - coastal Kenya
Luba - Zaire
Bemba - Zambia
Lunda -Zaire
Shona - Zimbabwe
Xhosa - South Africa

Cameroon man wearing ceremonial headdress

Bateke elder from the Congo

Zulu woman with typical hairstyle

Mouth of Zaire River

Mouth of Cuanza River

ATLANTIC OCEAN

Metal worker applying
gold leaf to a jewel

tered iron smelting. Those that knew smelting were able to acquire more fertile lands. They may have conquered the other groups they encountered because they had better weapons. Or they simply may have absorbed them into their societies.

The Bantu are found in and around forests, in the savanna, on mountain slopes, and on the fringes of semidesert areas in southern and eastern Africa. Due to the variety of Bantu habitats, it is nearly impossible to present one general picture of their culture. They generally lived in small villages. Their houses varied in style but were simply constructed. Men cleared fields, cut down trees in forested areas, hunted and skinned animals. The skins were used for trading or clothing. Bantu societies were patriarchal in nature, but women were mainstays of the community, responsible for growing and harvesting crops as well as running the household.

15

Omayyad warriors

Knight, on a bas-relief, in Cairo's Palace of the Fatimid Caliphs (11th–12th centuries) (Islamic Art Museum)

☐ Territory under Omayyad domination

☐ Islamic territory

☐ Territory under Fatimid domination

☐ Territory under Almoravid domination

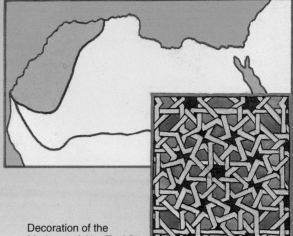

Decoration of the Madrasa of Abu Tashfin at Tlemcen (Morocco)

Muslim Dynasties in Africa

Elective Caliphate 632–661
Omayyad 661–750
Abbasid 750–1225

Rupture of Islamic unity
Egypt:
Tulunid 868–905
Fatimid 908–1171
Ayyubid 1171–1250
Mamluk 1250–1517
Ottoman 1517–1924

North Africa:
Aglabit (Central North Africa) 800–909
Almoravid (North Africa) 1056–1147
Almohad (North Africa) 1130–1269
Marinid (Morocco) 1248–1465
Hafsid (Tunisia) 1229–1545

The sequence of maps traces the conquest and direct Islamic domination of Egypt and North Africa and the spread of Islamic religious, cultural, and economic influence in the Sahara and Sahel regions, from the middle of the 7th century until the dominance of the Ottoman Empire in the 16th century.

There were six major periods during the Muslim conquest in the Mediterranean region of North Africa.
Omayyad; Fatimid; Almoravid
Almohad; Mamluk; Ottoman

The Arab Conquest heralded the start of the Middle Ages in Africa. Egypt was the first to be conquered, followed by the rest of the North African coast. Islam began to influence the religion, culture, and economics of North Africa.

The Islamic religion developed in Mecca, a trading city in Arabia. Its founder was the prophet Mohammed who, as a trader, probably had contact with both Jews and Christians. Like Judaism and Christianity, Islam is monotheistic (believing in one God). Muslims turn to the Koran rather than the Bible for divine guidance.

By Mohammed's death in A.D. 632, the Arabs were mostly united in the Islamic faith. They soon began to spread it through conquests made with their newly formed armies. They swept into Egypt, which was ruled by Byzantium in the east. By the early 600s, the Arabs had replaced the

The Mosque of Tinmallal, Almohad era

Ottoman warriors

■ Territory under Almohad domination

■ Territory under Mamluk domination

■ Territory under Ottoman domination

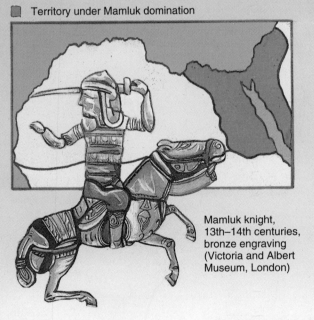

Mamluk knight, 13th–14th centuries, bronze engraving (Victoria and Albert Museum, London)

THE INFLUENCE OF ISLAM IN THE MEDITERRANEAN REGION OF AFRICA

unpopular Byzantines. Islam spread rapidly, and the Arabs attempted to move south into Nubia. They were repelled, however, and forced to set their boundary at the first cataract of the Nile.

The conquest of western North Africa was not easily accomplished. The Berbers, a nomadic people who had spread throughout North Africa, had never been subdued by the Byzantines. Thus the Arabs had to defeat first the Byzantines, then the Berbers, most of whom eventually yielded to the Arabs. With the Arab capital established in Tunis, their armies fanned out, reaching Morocco on the Atlantic coast by the early 700s.

The conquest of the Berbers did not mean that

they immediately converted to the religion of Islam. That came later through the work of missionaries from the east. The Berbers then became Islamic missionaries themselves, carrying the faith to sub-Saharan Africa.

Another group of easterners arrived in North Africa, as well. These newcomers were traders who eventually spread into sub-Saharan West Africa, buying gold and slaves from the middlemen there and selling items such as salt from the Sahara mines.

Conflict continued within parts of North Africa, much of it based on religious problems beyond the scope of this book. But we need to know that no single state was able to dominate all of western North

Africa. North Africa was always dominated by rulers based in Morocco and Tunisia, and Algeria continued to be a frontier area between the two. Numerous empires rose and fell between the 10th and 14th centuries. They were often the result of Islamic reform movements that proclaimed "holy wars" to reestablish the true faith. The history of Egypt was more straightforward, with power passing from the Fatimids to the Mamluks and finally to the Ottomans.

The events of the Islamic kingdoms in North Africa and particularly in Egypt are included here to complete the picture of African history and especially to stress their influence on the northern regions of sub-Saharan Africa.

WEST AFRICA

From the 9th century to the 16th, some of the most important nations in Africa's history developed in West Africa, just south of the Sahara Desert. These were the empires of Ghana, Mali, and Songhai. They were influenced by Islam but were not dominated by the nations in North Africa. The stability and level of development present in the area were very similar to those found in Europe and the Byzantine Empire at the beginning of the Middle Ages.

The Middle Ages, which most historians date from the 7th century to the 16th, was marked by prosperity, the spread of literacy in Arabic, and the further spread of Islam. Our knowledge of the empires of Ghana, Mali, and Songhai comes from Arab geographers who, again, relied on information supplied by merchants and other travelers. We also rely on oral traditions as well as more recent archeological digs. But in the cases of Mali and Songhai, we are able to draw on first-hand accounts of visitors. Ibn Battuta was in Mali for eight months in 1353, and Leo Africanus paid a diplomatic visit to Timbuktu between 1510 and 1520.

We have little in the way of information concerning West Africa before the Arab conquest of North Africa. The region was inhabited by a black population of mostly farmers and herders. Some were working in metals and others were mining gold. Toward the middle of the 8th century, because of increased trade across the Sahara, the desert became less of a barrier and more like a "sea of sand" which camel caravans increasingly crossed.

We do not know how long trade had existed across the Sahara with North Africa, but we do know that it increased when the Tuareg (a branch of the Berbers) began to move in, in search of gold. The Bambuk goldfields, as they were called,

Map showing the frontiers of the Ghana, Mali, and Songhai Empires

Ghana Empire borders

Mali Empire borders

Songhai Empire borders

Trade routes

Bronze razors engraved with the images of divinities (Carthage Museum)

Niger River

Granary of a typical Mande dwelling

(Far right) A wise man, a typical figure present in all stages of African history, especially in West Africa.

Longobard knight (taken from a bronze plaque in the Ticino region of Switzerland) and a knight thrown from his horse. Both date from the 7th century and may be compared with contemporary figures from the Empire of Ghana in West Africa.

Fortification typical of those found along the caravan routes

Woman wearing gold jewelry, bearing a basket

Solid gold necklace with ornamental objects

were hidden, and the local peoples maintained complete control over them.

All of the Sudanese empires indicated on the map developed at positions that enabled them to dominate the only trade routes existing between the north and south. The richest gold mining centers were located in the region between today's Senegal and the largest bend in the Niger River. Much of this area was within the territory of the Sudanese empires, but part of it also lay in the frontier regions to the south. It was therefore vital for these nations to maintain control over the southern routes and prevent people from the north from making direct contact with the mining areas.

The Atlantic coastline was difficult to reach. The trade winds were unfavorable to navigation. Even the Phoenician ships, which were the state-of-the-art vessels in ancient times, had never managed to return to their home ports. The waters of the coastline were also extremely shallow, with no natural ports where ships could anchor. This situation changed in the 15th century when the Portuguese developed a way of zigzagging slowly down the coast, which allowed them to sail south despite the prevailing winds. They anchored in deeper water and used small boats to row to land. The arrival of the Portuguese ships on the West African coasts coincided with events inland that marked the decline of the Sudanese empires. The new trade routes first opened by the Portuguese merchants were later used by the Dutch, French, English, Danes, and Swedes. Countries and cities along the coast of the Gulf of Guinea could then take advantage of new trade opportunities. The Europeans called these regions the Ivory Coast, Windward Coast, Gold Coast, and Slave Coast.

Ruins of the city and mosques of Awdaghost, discovered during recent archeological digs.

THE EMPIRE OF GHANA

The Empire of Ghana was an important kingdom located in West Africa, south of the Sahara Desert. The people in the area, the Soninke, were a branch of the Mande and as such were part of the Niger-Congo language group. They were probably farmers. Eventually the farming communities joined to form a kingdom located between the Niger and Senegal Rivers. Under successive chiefs, with superior weapons and using horses obtained from Saharan nomads, the Soninke conquered their weaker neighbors and created an empire.

The old Empire of Ghana is not to be confused with the contemporary country of Ghana, which is located farther south and on the Atlantic coast. Today's Ghana took the name of this monument to early African development. The capital of the Ghanian Empire was actually two cities, Kumbi and Saleh. Some experts believe that Kumbi was the political capital and Saleh the commercial center. The importance of Kumbi Saleh (as it is known today in Mauritania, where it is located) was its strategic location between the Bambuk goldfields on

The map shows the major caravan routes between the Empire of Ghana, Arab North Africa, and the region around Lake Chad; also Awdaghost, Kumbi, Niani, Gao, and Lake Chad.

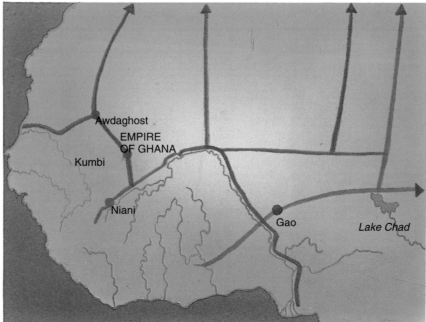

Artist's rendering of the city of Walata. The cities in these kingdoms were complex and built closely around the principal palaces and mosques. The dwellings were often huts made from flimsy building materials and wood.

Ceremonial shield and jewels made of gold

Princes and nobles of the court. Notice the elaborate headdresses they are wearing.

the upper Senegal River and the salt mines in the Sahara. By the mid-5th century, Ghana had grown in importance as trade between these areas increased. By the 9th century, Arabs from North Africa were regular visitors, although the Ghanians did not convert to Islam until much later.

Periodically over time, other Berbers to the north raided Ghana, meaning that traders were often robbed. As camel caravans increased in frequency, however, and as Ghana extended its borders, the trade routes became relatively peaceful. One reason why trade between the north and the south increased was that in the 9th and 10th centuries, North African kingdoms began to mint coins, which required more and more gold.

The kings of Ghana lived in splendor. Although they practiced their traditional religion until the 11th century, their contact with the Muslim world produced finery, such as brocade and silk from the east. The kings lived in what one account described as a palace. They were surrounded by the round huts of their administrators and followers, and nearby were the magicians who were responsible for religious affairs. The ancient Ghanians likely practiced matrilineage, meaning they traced their descent through their mothers rather than their fathers. Sons of the kings' sisters were eligible to inherit the throne and they, too, lived in relative luxury. The kings held court surrounded by slaves, conquered chiefs, and ministers. Petitioners from the kingdoms came on certain days to present their complaints directly to the kings, who also served as judges.

As with other past African societies, we know little about the common people in Ghana. Because oral traditions praised the kings, and because travelers were interested in kings and courts, almost no one reported on the day-to-day life of the empire's backbone. Most of the residents continued farming until they had overworked the land. Many were soldiers in the king's army. Some were artisans who made, among other things, the drums that were played when the king made his appearances and the jewelry worn by the royal families.

It is likely that few of the peasants ever converted to Islam. Or if they did, they mixed Islam with their traditional religion. This is called *syncretism* and was widely practiced among early converts to Islam, which has fewer required beliefs than Judaism or Christianity. Islam requires five basic beliefs, including the acceptance of only one God (Allah). Nevertheless, those who converted to Islam often clung to their own gods, as well. They felt secure in the religions they were raised with, since in nearly all African societies religion is an important part of the cultural values instilled in youth. This cultural factor will surface again when we discuss the kingdom of Songhai.

FROM THE FALL OF THE EMPIRE OF GHANA TO THE RISE OF THE MALI EMPIRE

Ruins of Kumbi Saleh, ancient capital of Ghana

Funeral urn found in the region of Timbuktu, proof of the widespread cult of ancestor worship

By the end of the 11th century, invasions from the Sosso people in the south, the rise of new trade routes, and overworking of the soil had ended Ghana's dominance. The empire eventually split up, but conflicts that arose in the region led to the rise of a new power, the Empire of Mali.

There is very little historical evidence of the period between the destruction of the capital of Ghana, Kumbi Saleh, in 1077 and the birth of the Mali Empire in 1235. This is an obscure period of west Sudanese history and all we know has come from the oral tradition and from objects and ruins found during archeological digs. Kumbi Saleh was destroyed by Abubakar, leader of the Almoravids, and his men. The Almoravids had conquered and dominated the whole of North Africa and part of the Empire of Ghana proclaiming a holy war to force a return to the more original forms of Islam.

The Almoravids directly controlled a large part of the area previously the Empire of Ghana for only about a decade. They imposed Islam but never really managed to reestablish the past economic and commercial strength of the region. They failed to dominate the old vassal states touching the borders of the ex-Empire of Ghana, many of which achieved their independence. A fresh struggle between these newly independent states began in the race for regional supremacy.

Among the smaller kingdoms emerging from the Empire of Ghana was Kingui, later named Diara after its capital. In the early 12th century, the Kingui were also overthrown by the Sosso, who reestablished the traditional religion and attempted to check the spread of Islam by conquering back all of what was the Empire of Ghana.

Sosso domination of the former empire was short-lived, and around the beginning of the 13th century other Mande-speaking peoples pushed west toward Senegambia (the area in west Africa around the Senegal and Gambia Rivers); eastward to gain control of the city-state of Hausa, in today's Nigeria; and south to the regions just inland from the coastal strip of Guinea.

Djerma Songhai women from Balayera (Niger) and Soninke (Mauritania)

A magnificent 4-inch-long pendent found in the Middle Niger region (Mali), showing the figure of a woman; the meaning of her position is unknown.

Swamp near Sanga, a village 30 miles northeast of Bandjagara

Landscape at the top, and below:

Map of the ancient Mande kingdom southwest of Bamako (UNESCO Foundation)

Map labels:
Mande Hills
Soso
Dodugu
KIRI
Bamako
Kiri
Sibi
Niger River
Dakadiala
Tabon
Narena
Djiguidala
BAKO
Badagu Djeliba
Kankaba
BURE
Tigan
Sankarani River
Selegon
Kankari
Milo River
Niani
Djelibakore
Balanduguba
WASULU
Amana
Kamaro
Barro
Kankan

Dogon bronze and brass sculpture of a group of Dogan knights, among the most important noblemen of the empire

Old Manding

The ancient land of the Mande peoples, Old Manding, stretched from the high, wet tablelands of Baule and Bafing on one side to the valley of the Niger River on the other. This was a savanna region where cereals, rice, and vegetables were grown. Their methods of cultivation were so advanced that someone suggested the Mande peoples had a particular gift for agriculture. After examining a large number of farming tools found in several areas, however, it seems more likely to historians that the Sahara and the Sudan, together with Egypt and the Near East, were part of a single process of agricultural development. In any case the Mande played an important part in the development of agriculture in Africa. It was they who probably introduced the African variety of rice to the region.

The rise of the Mali Empire was greatly helped by its control of the gold deposits along the southern boundaries of the region. Its position near the gold deposits was even more favorable than the ancient Empire of Ghana's had been. Arab scholars of the times left little information about the ancient land of the Mande before the time of Sundiata and the rise of Mali.

The bust of a bearded man

Bandjagara, a typical example of a Dogon village perched on slopes; the Dogon peoples lived south of the Niger in the basin formed by the White Volta and Black Volta Rivers

Dugout canoes on the Niger River

Landscapes of the savanna, near Bamako (Niger)

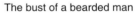

23

SUNDIATA AND THE CREATION OF THE MALI EMPIRE

The discovery of new goldfields shifted trade to the west and helped lead to the emergence of the Malinke kingdom of Mali. At its height, the empire stretched from the Atlantic coast of today's Senegambia to Gao, the capital of Songhai. Mali extended southward from the desert's edge to include the Bure goldfields, with its capital Niani located nearby.

The Malinke, like the Soninke, were Mande speakers. The Sosso who had conquered part of Ghana were Soninke, which meant their language also was derived from Mande. Although these ethnic groups were distant relatives, they had developed separate languages and somewhat different cultures, and they were frequently at odds with each other.

As Ghana declined, conflict developed in the region between the Soninke, Sosso, and Malinke who lived to the south. The groups made raids on one another, and a Malinke leader—named Sundiata—arose from this chaos. Sundiata formed an army and, in 1235, defeated the Soninke peoples who had been conquered by the Sosso. This forced the Sosso into retreat and allowed Sundiata to begin building the immense Empire of Mali.

The story of Sundiata's rise to power and his success in building the empire has been handed down generation to generation among speakers of Mande. In the following passages we are treated to an example of the oral tradition. Oral traditions often change over time, however, and are somewhat dependent on who is telling them, so we should note that what we know for certain about Sundiata's origin is that he was a member of the Keita clan of the Malinke.

The oral tradition comes to us from the national anthem of the modern Republic of Mali. The story

Earthenware Dogon sculpture of a male figure wearing snakes, symbol of the link between humans and the spiritual world

The village of Kirina, one of the cities at the center of the Mali Empire and the place where Sundiata defeated his rival Sumanguru in 1235

Earthenware pottery for everyday use and stemmed funeral urns found during the excavations in Niani

(Bottom) Pot used for collecting milk in Fulani (Peul); the complicated decoration has a religious meaning.

Niani, capital of the Mali Empire; shown is a section of the city reconstructed after recent archeological excavations.

begins with Sundiata as the son of Narin Famakhan, king of the Malinke and one of his wives, Sogolon Kudiuma. The song is a hymn of joy celebrating the recovery of the nine-year-old boy who had been paralyzed, but had always defended his mother from the king's family. This was necessary because Sundiata's mother was considered unattractive and was the subject of ridicule. His recovery was attributed to magic powers. According to oral tradition, Sundiata became famous in his youth for his exceptional strength and skills as a hunter and warrior.

When the old king died, one of Sundiata's stepbrothers, Dankuma Tuma, took the throne. He was jealous of Sundiata and exiled him and his mother. During this exile, Sundiata became an even greater warrior, and his fame spread. When the Malinke kingdom was attacked by the Sosso, the king proved unable to organize his country's defense. Because of his reputation as a warrior, the people called Sundiata back to defend his native land. During the long and difficult struggle Sundiata was able to gain the support of several brave generals, and together they defeated the intruder Sumanguru at the battle of Kirina.

This is a shortened version of the legend of Sundiata, but it does contain some true facts. The story of his sudden recovery makes us suppose that Sundiata was not only a great warrior, but also was regarded as a kind of priest or magician. The Mali Empire was probably a sort of feudal federation made up of different peoples. Sundiata appointed the generals who had helped him win the battle of Kirina (in about 1235) to rule each of these kingdoms.

The Malinke kings were thought to have magical powers. They could be said to head both church and state, except in the case of the Malinke "church" meant the traditional religion, based on a combination of ancestor worship and worship of the spirits that controlled the land. Since the Malinke were primarily farmers, regular rains and fertile soil were essential to their livelihood. The Malinke also kept livestock. Like the Ghanians, some of the townspeople were artisans, some were slaves, and during Sundiata's reign, many men were in the army. But the primary economic activity was gold mining. The gold deposits as well as the trade they produced allowed Mali to extend its boundaries, pay its army, and serve as the major trading center in West Africa during much of the 13th and 14th centuries.

As the hub for all exchange between north and south, Mali produced a group of traders who, though Muslim, were local Soninke or Malinke men. They began to fan out from Niani during Sundiata's reign, bringing trade goods from the north into unchartered areas of West Africa. These Dyula traders, as they are called in many parts of West Africa, can be found today as far away as Gabon and Angola and the interior of central Africa.

The kings of Mali, had administrators who collected taxes in the form of agricultural produce. They also taxed all trade goods that passed into and out of the empire. The kings were held in great respect and acted as judges of last resort. Many who followed Sundiata were nominally Muslim, but most of the people still regarded them as leaders of the traditional religion in spite of their supposed conversion.

THE MALI EMPIRE AFTER SUNDIATA

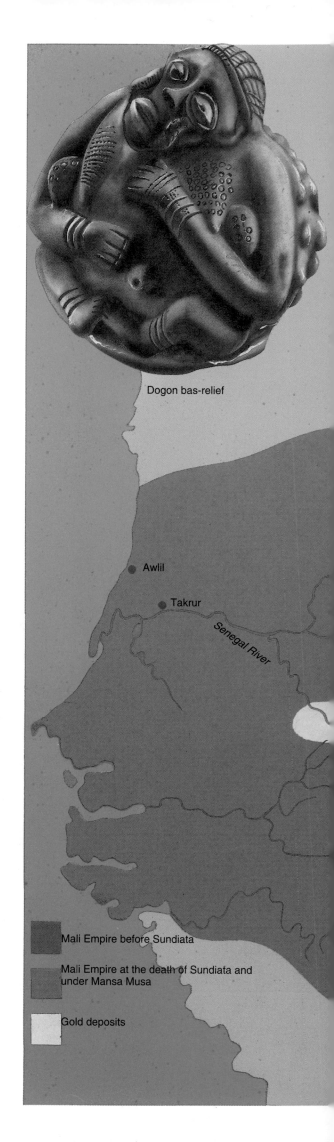

Dogon bas-relief

Awlil

Takrur

Senegal River

Mali Empire before Sundiata

Mali Empire at the death of Sundiata and under Mansa Musa

Gold deposits

Sundiata's most famous successor was Mansa Musa the First. He is the only sovereign in history to be remembered for a pilgrimage instead of his military or administrative achievements. His glittering pilgrimage to Cairo and Mecca, an Islamic holy city, was famous throughout the Muslim world and even across Europe.

Mali was a vast empire at this time. Apart from Niani, other cities had developed along the main trade routes. Timbuktu and Gao, with their buildings made from mud and strengthened with wooden beams, were typical examples of Sudanese architecture.

The dark violet shading on the map shows the early center of the empire; the lighter violet shows the size of the empire at the death of Sundiata and under Mansa Musa, and the areas shaded in yellow are the regions containing gold deposits.

Mansa Musa's Pilgrimage to Mecca

Sundiata's immediate successors were less important then he had been. However, Mali reached the height of its power during the reign of Mansa Musa from 1312–37. A devout Muslim, Mansa Musa set off for Mecca, the Islamic holy city and destination of pilgrimages, in 1324 with a caravan so large it included around 100 camels whose sole cargo was gold. His pilgrimage lasted two years and was so impressive that word of Mali's emperor reached Europe as well as North Africa and, of course, Arabia, where he traveled after a lengthy stopover in Cairo. While Mansa Musa and his party were in Cairo, they spent lavishly from their horde of gold, causing inflation that lasted long after their departure. The Arab historian Ibn Kaldun recorded that the Malian king was accompanied to Mecca by several wives, princes, dignitaries, and griots, together with an army of several thousand men.

The famous pilgrimage had political and economic effects and marked the shift of the traditional caravan routes farther eastward, particularly in the direction of Egypt. Traffic with the North African area of Morocco slowed as that region began to decline. Niani, Timbuktu, Gao, and Djenne became important centers of trade and culture.

Musa's generosity attracted scholars and literary figures to Mali from Egypt and Arabia. They were given the task of spreading Islam systematically throughout the kingdom. Timbuktu became the seat of an important school, while new palaces and mosques were built in the principal cities, giving rise to what became known as the Sudanese style of architecture. Practice of the traditional religion remained widespread, however. The king himself would have been unwise to forbid it as he would have lost much of his power over the people.

The Mali Empire was at its largest under Mansa Musa. It extended from the Atlantic Ocean in the west to Tadmekka in the east and from the salt mines of Teghazza in the Sahara to the forest region farther south. There were about 400 cities in all. Mansa Musa promoted a peaceful foreign policy and friendly relations with bordering countries. Unfortunately the empire had become too large to be effectively controlled from the center. By the end of the 14th century, the Mali Empire was clearly in decline. The weakness of Mansa's successors was certainly partly to blame, but this was not the only cause. Attacks by the kingdoms from the south, together with attacks by groups of Tuaregs from the desert on the city of Timbuktu weakened the empire further. The final blow was dealt by the rulers of Gao. After destroying the Mali capital of Niani they founded a new kingdom, the Songhai Empire, which was in direct competition with the Empire of Mali. Mali survived until 1645, a small state ruled by the Keita Dynasty, but never regained its past splendor.

Carved wooden tablet from Nupe (Nigeria); tablets like this were normally used to protect sacred texts such as the Koran.

Tuareg warrior riding his white dromedary

Teghazza

Ibn Batuta's Observations on the Importance of Justice in the Mali Empire

Following is a list of some of the fine qualities noted by this Arab scholar on his travels through the Mali Empire: **1.** Very few unjust acts are to be seen because among all peoples the Africans are those who most hate injustice. **2.** Mali is a very safe place. Residents and travelers alike have nothing to fear from thieves. **3.** Africans never confiscate even the most valuable property of white men who die in their country. **4.** They take their religion very seriously, they pray and practice religious rituals with care and punish their children for forgetting their religious duties. **5.** They wear white each Friday. Those who only have one shirt or tunic launder it carefully ready to take part in public prayers. **6.** They are very keen on learning the Koran by heart.
(taken from Book 4 of Ibn Batuta's Travels)

Djinger-Ber Mosque (Timbuktu), built by Mansa Musa in the 14th century, and totally rebuilt in the 17th century

Walata

Timbuktu

Gao

Askia Mohammed's tomb in Gao (Mali, 16th century)

Outer walls of the Jenne Mosque (Mali), built by Mansa Musa in the 14th century

Dia

Kukya

Niger River

Jenne

Kirina

Bani River

Niger River

Kankaba

Kiri

Dakadiala

Niani

Kouroussa

Woman from northern Nigeria; her elaborate hairstyle and jewels are symbols of her high caste.

THE MANDE CIVILIZATION

Both the Empire of Ghana and, more especially, the Mali Empire were forms of the Mande civilization. They were typified by a complex political and administrative organization based on a balance between partially centralized and partially decentralized power. The sovereign or "mansa" represented this power but was limited in its absolute use by ancient traditions and by the laws of Islam. For his strength he depended on his army and on the collection of taxes and tolls levied on the camel caravans crossing his territory.

Despite being a rich country, Mali did not mint its own currency. Instead it used different goods for money, such as gold, copper, salt, and even special kinds of shells, or Arab coins like dinars and kintars.

Mali's society was organized exactly as it had been in the Empire of Ghana, and Islam remained the official religion. As in the past, however, the majority of people were animists, those who worship inanimate objects or objects in nature.

At the height of its influence, the Mali Empire dominated the entire region of Sudan and west Sahel.

This vast area included very different groups of peoples and cultures: for example, groups such as the Tuareg desert people who controlled the important salt mines of Taghaza and Jil. The Tuareg were very different from their neighbors, such as those whose activities were based on agriculture and growing cereals or those who bred livestock. One of the most studied ethnic groups are the Dogon. They were especially famous for their creativity and craftsmanship.

The Mali Empire enjoyed political stability for over two centuries. The centralized power represented by the sovereign, his court, his officials, and dignitaries in Niani managed to balance out the independence of the provinces, which were often linked to the center by a strong but almost symbolic bond.

In this way Mali was both an empire and a confederation. Even if the great Mande had formed alliances with the king, they retained their freedom. The king was Muslim even though he still kept the role granted him by traditional religion. He was polygamous, meaning he had several wives, but his first wife enjoyed a position of special importance

and had certain powers. The new king had to be enthroned sitting on the hide of a freshly killed bull, which was then used to make the royal drum, symbol of the king's power.

According to Ibn Batutta, the Mali court was lavish and bound by strict rules of etiquette. The king granted audience while sitting under a special dome. All requests had to be addressed to one of his intermediaries: only they had the right to speak to him. His prime minister was one of these intermediaries: He was chosen directly by the king, usually from among the griots.

Musician playing the ardin, a stringed instrument

Council chamber, also called the "Great Shelter," for the men in a Dogon village. The cane roof is supported by massive wooden pillars, decorated with symbols representing the male and female elements in creation.

The commoners, on the other hand, were governed by the *farin* or *farba* who was nominated (or dismissed) by the king. The subordinate provinces kept their local rulers, who had to provide squads of soldiers for the mansa's army. The system was not completely feudal, as no funds were involved either from the king or the local leaders, but it stood the test of time. Contemporary Arab sources spoke admiringly of the high level of security and strong sense of justice present everywhere in the Mali Empire.

Mali's economy was based on agriculture, a prosperous craft industry, and exploitation of the country's mineral wealth—salt in the north—gold, iron, and copper in the south. The Mali Empire resembled the earlier Empire of Ghana, but its territory was much greater. The society was characterized by a very rigid class system, including an aristocracy made up of scholars, dignitaries, and public officials, and a dynamic middle class involved in commercial activities.

Islam was the religion of the aristocracy while the peasants were usually animists. The schools founded in the mosques and palaces were vibrant cultural centers. The ruins of these buildings show the importance of the empire's architecture. Music and dance were extremely popular as the variety and sophistication of musical instruments dating back to this era demonstrate.

Head of a Fulani (or Peul) woman, from northern Nigeria; notice the typical hairstyle and hooped earrings.

Interior of a Tuareg tent with its huge bed, and a shield, or "worudwadji," made from the skin of the animal bearing the same name. In the foreground we can see a Tuareg silversmith.

A village mosque in Mali, in the region between San and Mopti

Fulani children from the Djelgobe group (Burkina Faso), taking water from a pond with a "ghirbe," a kind of container made from goatskins

Narrow dugout canoes typical of the Niger River

THE SONGHAI EMPIRE AND OTHER WEST SUDANESE KINGDOMS

The Mali Empire collapsed because it became too large to rule and its frontiers were too far from the center for the king to control them effectively. A new empire, the Songhai Empire, was established. It was located farther east to correspond with the eastern shift of the routes crossing the Sahara, away from the increasingly restless region of Morocco.

Mali was overthrown by internal rebellions and anarchy because its territory had become too vast for the king to dominate with his army, and the Songhai kings dealt the final blow. The new empire made exactly the same mistakes, however, failing to organize both the economy and society effectively. This empire also expanded too rapidly and became so large that the king was regarded as

a total foreigner by the majority of his subjects who sought to free themselves from his domination.

The Songhai nation extended all along the course of the Niger River, giving cultural unity to the region. The large number of archeological finds made in this area shows that it was inhabited from prehistoric times. The Mali emperor, Mansa Musa, conquered the area and made it a vassal state. At that time he captured two local princes, taking them back to his court as hostages. The oral tradition tells the story of their eventual escape and return to their own land. There they formed the Sonni Dynasty and began the struggle against their powerful neighbor. Sonni Ali the Great (1464–1492) was the founder of the Songhai Empire, the Sundiata of the north. His

army gradually invaded the tributary territories of the Mali Empire, forcing them to become vassal states of the Songhai Empire. One by one the Dogon, the Mossi, the Fulani (or Peul), and the desert Tuaregs were all defeated by the Songhai army. The siege of the city Dienne on the Niger River was particularly spectacular. It was carried out by a floating armada which came up the river.

During the war Sonni Ali had reestablished the traditional religion in Timbuktu, much to the dismay of the local *ulemas*, important experts on the Muslim faith. Sonni Ali was succeeded by Askia Mohammed (1493–1528), who reestablished Islam in Timbuktu to help strengthen his position and to use the organizational and administrative advantages offered by

Tuareg warriors

Caravan transporting salt from the Qualata Mines in Mauritania

View of the city of Moudjeria (Mauritania), built near an oasis on the northern edge of the Sahel; today the city has almost disappeared.

Islam. To mark this conversion he undertook a pilgrimage to the Muslim holy shrines and was granted the title of Caliph by the Great Sharif of Mecca. Later he became blind and was deposed by his sons. After Askia Mohammed's death the country was thrown into confusion by internal wars, then conquered by the Marinid sultan of Morocco at the end of the 16th century. At the height of its influence, the Songhai Empire stretched from the border with Morocco in the northern Sahara to the frontier with Kanem Bornu in the east, and roughly from the Senegal River in the west to the region of Hambori to the south. The center of the empire shifted toward the east, a process already begun during the time of the Mali Empire. This coincided with the increase in power of the more central North African kingdoms and the declining influence of the more turbulent region of Morocco.

South of the large bend in the Niger River, in the Volta River region, lived another important people, the Mossi. They were clever farmers and enjoyed the advantage of a more fertile savanna region than the one found in Mali. They were separated into three fairly large kingdoms, among them Ouagadougou, the capital of today's Burkina Faso. The Mossi were profoundly traditional in their religion, and resisted the influence of Islam. They organized themselves into rural societies headed by a monarch, preserving their independent form of civilization until the French conquest in the 19th century.

The Fulani people (or Peul, as the French call them) are among the most typical populations of the Western Sahara region. They are present in various areas from the Sahara to Central Africa. Their origin is unknown. They were, and many still are, primarily nomad shepherds, famous for their beauty and courage. A small group may have emigrated following the orders of a clan chief. The Fulani were always searching for better pastures to feed their herds. Perhaps a few limited groups decided to settle in one area and founded small kingdoms which were later dominated, first by the Mali Empire and afterward by the Empire of Songhai. Neither of these two empires managed to absorb the culture or destroy it.

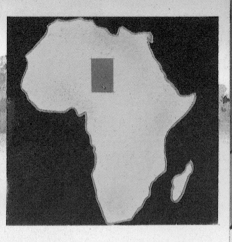

Map showing peoples and kingdoms
in the Chad area (14th century)

To Wargia
To Tripoli
To Egypt
FEZZAN
Zawila
Ghat
TUBU
Diado
KAWAR
al-Kasaba
To Gao
TUWA RIK
Bilma
Takedda
Aghram
Dunes and desert regions
KANEM
TUBU
HAUSA
Djimi
MUNIO
Zamtam
Yao
Lake Chad
Diakam
Makari
BORNU
BAGIRMI

Typical view of Lake Chad and its islands, with
the village of Zaghawa and its characteristic
cone-shaped roofs in the foreground

This region is named after Lake Chad, a huge lake, the remains of an even larger internal sea present during prehistoric times. Lake Chad is situated almost at the center of a wide depression, with the dunes from the desert stretching from the north to the lake's shores and is surrounded by savanna land to the south, east, and west. Small communities of fishermen and livestock breeders live on the islands in the center of the lake. Along its shores we find merchants, caravan leaders, and desert herdsmen.

The vast region of the Lake Chad basin and Lake Chad depression collects all the waters in the area. During prehistoric times the large inland sea probably had a densely populated coastline, until the climate changed and the Sahara became arid and inhospitable. This process ended around 2500–2000 B.C. The size of the lake was drastically reduced and the climate became much less livable. To the north lay arid desert and to the south, a savanna region of bushes and the occasional tree.

Artifacts of the Sao Civilization: Fort Lamy, Chad; the Courtin Excavations; pottery found during the excavations.

Statuette in the Tago Sanctuary (Chad), probably a likeness of the first inhabitants of the area who have now completely disappeared

CHAD, THE CROSSROADS OF AFRICA

But these factors did not deter the gradual arrival of new populations to the Chad region. They came from areas that had become totally inhospitable for climatic, political, or military reasons. These peoples were very different from each other, having different languages and cultures. In particular they were Berber nomad shepherds, fishermen, or farmers. Perhaps they even included the legendary Sao people—traditionally a population of giants, famous for their strength. In the oral tradition, the name Sao often indicates populations that existed previously, were difficult to assimilate, and were totally eliminated over time.

The most recent archeological finds seem to indicate that these different peoples who settled in the Chad region one after the other became neither unified nor intermingled. This is probably due to their very different levels of development. The arrival of these peoples and their efforts to adapt to their new environment form the background to the history of Chad, which began around the 11th century but gained real importance only toward the 12th and 13th centuries.

The Caravan Routes

Two important caravan routes ended in the Chad region. They were opened up as camels began to be used for transportation, which was so vital to the history of the Sahara. The route that pushed farthest to the east—the Darb el Arbein—led a caravan from Egypt to Darfur in 40 days' march and then turned to the northeast point of the lake. The second was the shortest route from the Tunisian ports to Lake Chad by way of the oasis of Kaouar. There was a third but less important route, which followed the valleys west of the Nile River in the direction of the lake. The control and administration of these routes were gradually taken over by the Arab and Berber populations forced to flee from Egypt or Arabia. They were most likely refugees who arrived in successive waves to the area, gradually assuming military and political control. This process resulted in the establishment of the Kingdom of Kanem in the 9th century. This was followed by the rise of the combined

kingdoms of Kanem, on the northeast of Lake Chad; and Bornu, which was southwest of the lake and founded in the late 13th century. We shall examine Kanem Bornu shortly.

As in West Africa, power and prestige were gained by controlling the caravan routes to and from the north and those crossing the dense tropical forests to the south. Huge empires like the Ghana, Mali, and Songhai Empires in West Sudan did not develop, however. This was probably because the peoples who settled the area were so different and because the area was so difficult to control. Kanem was probably founded by nomad clans whose wealth came, in part, from trading slaves in the south for horses. While Kanem emerged as a Muslim state of some significance in the 13th century, Bornu was not a force of any importance until the 15th century when Kanem was beginning to decline. The leaders of Bornu traded with the Akan peoples to the south (today's Ghana) and with the Hausa in the west, serving as middlemen between these black African peoples and the Fezzan in the north.

A village near the city of Kano (now in northern Nigeria); in the foreground are women collecting water in typical pottery jars, and in the background are two domed granaries made from dried mud and a hut made today using exactly the same building methods as in the past

THE KINGDOMS OF CHAD AND THE NIGERIA REGION

There are three main influences in the history of this area: iron, which was responsible for the development of better armor; the horse; and the camel, which were used for transportation or for fighting. Several of the most important caravan routes to and from the Mediterranean ports of Tunisia and Libya terminated to the north of Lake Chad. To the south of the lake was the starting point of trade routes with the states along the Guinea coast and the forest regions between central Sudan and northern Congo.

Ife Art

The state of Ife in Nigeria was founded sometime around the 11th or 12th century. Like the Mande speakers, the Yoruba were of the Niger-Congo language group. Before the founding of their first kingdom in Ife, the Yoruba lived in small villages where they farmed, traded, and hunted. An elaborate artistic tradition developed in Ife. It produced sculptures first in stone and later in bronze, copper, and wood. The stone sculptures, of which only a few remain, were probably created in the 13th century. The later sculptures were done with the lost wax method, which meant that no two pieces were ever the same.

Ife artists also worked with baked clay. This tradition of creating terra-cotta statues goes back to the Nok culture in central Nigeria at least since 400 B.C.

The Nigerian Region

The Nok culture is also linked with the old kingdom of Benin, which was located in central Nigeria. By 1500 the kingdom of Benin stretched from the Niger Delta in the east to Lagos, on the Atlantic in the west. The artists of Benin worked in terra-cotta, and also created magnificent, naturalistic sculptures in bronze, wood, and copper.

Ife art from Nigeria (12th–14th century); a 16-inch-high bronze figure of an Ife *oni* or king, in ceremonial costume decorated with royal symbols

The influence of the "Sudanese" model of civilization, together with its distinctive type of political organization, spread across regions which were geographically outside the true Sudan region. Toward the end of the first 1,000 years A.D., a series of Hausa city-states were founded in the area between present-day northern Nigeria and the Republic of Niger. There were several major city-states: Kano, Zaria, Gobir, Katsina, and Kebbi. There were even more minor ones. They were probably founded by groups who had emigrated from the Chad region, and they reached a high level of development due to a strong economy based on farming, livestock breeding, handicrafts, and trade.

The slave trade was also important to the Hausa city-states. Some slaves were kept to work as farmers or builders, while the trade itself brought prosperity. The merchants who traded in slaves also brought Islam to the Hausa in the 14th century.

The influence of the Hausa city-states probably extended south, toward the Upper Volta region situated at the center of the wide bend in the Niger River. Three important kingdoms were founded here by the Mossi peoples between the 11th and 15th centuries.

To the south, in the area covered by present-day central and western Nigeria, the Yoruba peoples created their original civilization. The wealth and sophistication of Benin are clearly described in the records of the first Portuguese navigators to reach these coasts at the end of the 15th century.

The Akan and the Kingdom of Ashanti

A few hundred miles south of the Mossi area and west of the Volta River, the Akan people emerged. By the 16th century they had formed several states, including the Fante on the coast, and the Ashanti in what is today central Ghana. The Akan were farmers until they discovered gold in the forests where they hunted game. Then, some of the Akan became miners, staking out the gold mines as personal property. This new-found source of wealth enabled the owners to become chiefs who then presided over the states that developed nearby.

When the Portuguese came to the coast in the late 15th century they traded with the Akan. In exchange for their gold and slaves that came from Benin, the Akan received cotton, metals, and later, guns. The Portuguese also introduced new agricultural products from Brazil, including corn.

In the mid-17th century the Ashanti kingdom was founded by Osei Tutu. He located his capital in Kumasi and conquered other Akan, spreading Ashanti rule to the gold mines. Osei Tutu was followed by Opuku Ware in the early 18th century. He continued Ashanti conquests so that by 1750 they controlled almost all of the territory of contemporary Ghana. Osei Tutu as king was called the *asantehene*. According to the oral tradition, the heavens opened and a golden stool dropped at his feet. This meant that he was chosen by divine sources, which gave him

religious authority as well as secular power. His successors, who were chosen by each old king before he died or a council of Ashanti leaders, and who were usually related to the old *asantehene*, were presented with the golden stool when they assumed office.

Slavery was widely practiced among the Ashanti. It was the slaves who performed most of the labor in the gold mines and who composed the lower ranks in the army. The Ashanti peasants continued farming although many of them were also involved in aspects of gold mining, and others were traders who carried the gold to the coast or elsewhere. The gold mines were controlled by the Akan peoples and no outsiders were allowed into the capital until the British arrived in the 19th century.

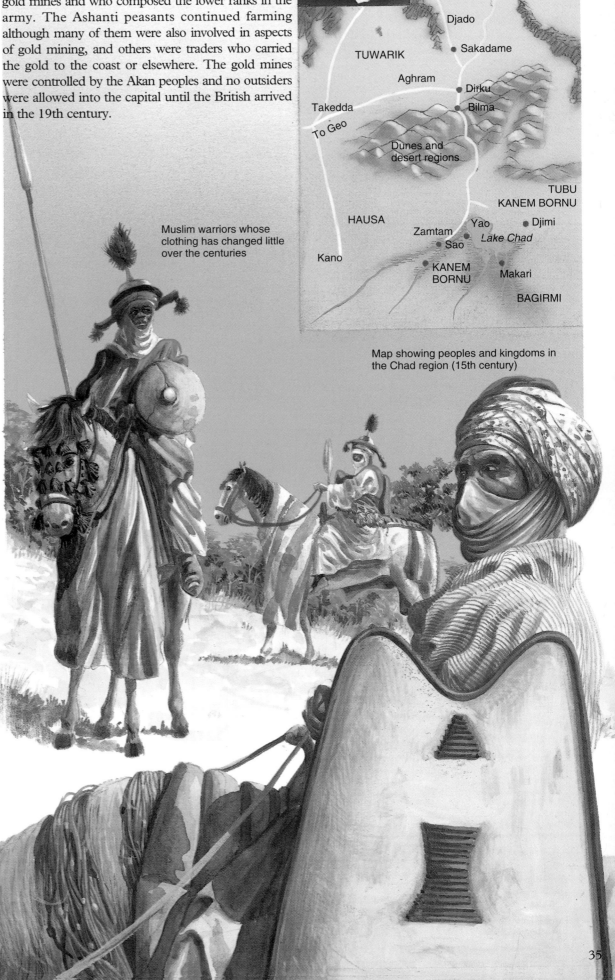

Muslim warriors whose clothing has changed little over the centuries

Map showing peoples and kingdoms in the Chad region (15th century)

35

NUBIA AND ETHIOPIA: REGIONS RESISTANT TO THE MUSLIM CONQUEST

At the beginning of the 13th century, during the reign of Lalibela, the Kingdom of Ethiopia in east Africa enjoyed a period of renaissance and splendor. Twelve outstanding early Christian churches constructed in the capital Zague, later renamed Lalibela, are a reminder of this period of Ethiopian history. The churches and convents were built in remote places but became centers for pilgrimages and education for the religious and political leaders of the country.

Nubia is the region of the Nile cataracts, south of Egypt. During the last 1,000 years B.C., it was the area where the ancient Kush civilization developed, centered on the two capitals, Napata and Meroe. After being conquered by the Axum Empire, situated farther south on the southern shores of the Red Sea, Kush changed its name to Nubia. Around the 6th century, the Monophysite, or Coptic, form of Christianity spread here from Egypt. This branch of Christianity believes in Christ only as a divine being, rejecting the idea that he had a human nature, as well. It developed and grew strong enough to resist the Islamic conquest of Egypt.

In the 8th century, a treaty of nonaggression was signed between the Arabs and the Nubians. The conditions of the treaty included the exchange of 360 young Nubian slaves in return for Egyptian horses, cloth, and grain; the construction of a mosque in Dongola—the principal city in Nubia—and the guarantee of religious freedom for Muslims living in Nubia. Nubia was also guaranteed religious and political independence.

The treaty last for seven centuries, apart from a few isolated incidents like the raid organized by the Nubian king Kyriatos to free the Patriarch of Alexandria from prison. Unfortunately most of the archeological sites still waiting to be discovered and studied to teach us more about this region were destroyed during the construction of the Aswan Dam.

In the late 14th century, the small Christian kingdoms in Nubia fell to Islam. The most important of these was the Kingdom of Dongola. This was the beginning of the split between Muslims and Christians still present in the state of Sudan today.

The Coptic Christian Church in Ethiopia resisted Islam longer than the Church in Nubia. This was the region of the important Axum Empire. In ancient times the area was famous for the great port of Adulis. Adulis was one of the trade centers on the Red Sea, together with those founded by the Greeks, Romans, Byzantines, and Persians.

(Above, right) View of the top of St. George's Church, Lalibela

The Ethiopian plateau; herd grazing and a man collecting firewood

Eastern view of the church and monastery of Faras (Nubia), surrounded by Arab fortifications

The city walls of Faras, rebuilt with ancient materials

Typical vertical wooden funeral monument made by the Konso peoples of Ethiopia

At first Axum was dominated by the rulers of southern Arabia, but gradually it became more independent and its sovereign took the title "king of kings." The language that emerged, Ge'ez, is still used today in the Orthodox Ethiopian churches. Ge'ez was followed by Amharic, which the people of Ethiopia speak. Both languages are of the Afro-Asiatic group. Christianity began to spread across the region in the 4th century, probably brought by missionaries from eastern Europe. There were several reasons for Axum's eventual decline. Trade between the Mediterranean areas and India decreased. Commercial shipping routes in the Mediterranean were interrupted by the Muslim conquests. At the beginning of the 8th century, the Arabs destroyed the port of Adulis. Now Ethiopia was isolated from the Christian world not only geographically, but also religiously because it remained faithful to the Coptic form of Christianity. A long period of decline began during which the nation had to concentrate all its efforts on defending itself from Muslim attacks from the coast and assaults along its southern borders from the Oromo Galla people. This situation lasted for several centuries. Over time the military leaders became feudal rulers.

Around the 13th century there was a brief return to unity, when the ras, or ruler, of the province of Shoa dominated the other local rulers for a short time. He proclaimed the rebirth of the "Dynasty of Solomon." In a certain sense, this marked the beginning of modern history in Ethiopia, which continued an even more determined struggle against the spread of Islam and made every effort to convert the pagan population to Christianity. The early Christian churches in Ethiopia bear witness to this period of resistance and are indeed some of the architectural wonders of the African continent.

During this period the system of dividing the land into three parts began. One part was given to the king and his family, one to the convents, and one to the people. This created the basis of the political and social resistance to change typical of Ethiopian society until the upheavals of the 1970s.

Toward the end of the 15th century, the Portuguese began to take an interest in Ethiopia. They convinced the "negus" (ruler) to sign a treaty of alliance. The Portuguese presence helped Ethiopia to resist the threat of invasion by the Turks, but at the same time it allowed Jesuit missionaries into the country. They tried in vain to oppose the Coptic form of Christianity and were driven out of Ethiopia in the 17th century. By this time the country had entered a period of decline.

Tomb of Sheik Hussein, 13th century Islamic prophet (Bale Province, Ethiopia; Mandebo Mountains near the source of the Uebi Scebeli River). This prophet was the first representative of Islam to penetrate the Ethiopian plateau area from the south by following the river upstream to its source. A sanctuary was built here and is the destination of two annual pilgrimages, particularly for the Galla peoples. They are herders, and during religious celebrations they decorate the prophet's tomb with lengths of brightly colored cloth.

Map showing the position of the Ethiopian plateau

THE INDIAN OCEAN: CULTURE AND COMMERCE; LINK BETWEEN EAST AFRICA AND ASIA

It has often been said that the history of the East African coastline is better thought of as the history of the western shores of the Indian Ocean. From the 7th century A.D., Arab influence began to spread across the Indian Ocean. The Arabs, however, like the Persians, Indians, and other seagoing peoples of the Orient, were almost exclusively interested in the islands and coastal regions of East Africa. Many city-states developed in these areas, but not in the arid and almost unpopulated inland regions. These regions, however, were important for the supply of precious metals—chiefly gold—ivory, and slaves.

The African coast from Cape Guardafui in the north to the mouth of the Zambesi River in the south is dominated by the monsoon winds that blow in a southerly direction in the winter and toward the north in the summer. These winds allowed contact and trade with other Asian regions facing the Indian Ocean. The inland regions supplied many of the goods to be exchanged, but no important overland trade routes were developed in the area until the 19th century. There were several reasons for this. First, the area was arid and hostile to development, rather like a natural barrier. But second and perhaps more important, the coastal populations were extremely focused on their activities linked to the trade networks up to the Red Sea coast and crossing the Indian Ocean.

Two important ancient historical sources help us to understand early events in this area. They are "The Periplus of the Erythraean Sea," a navigational guide used by sailors during the first century A.D., and "Geography" by Claudius Ptolemy, dating back to the second century A.D. but probably modified two centuries later. These sources seem to suggest the existence of flourishing trade, especially in ivory, as far back as the time of the Roman Empire, between the 1st and the 4th centuries A.D.

We have no direct written, and little archeological evidence dealing with the period from the 4th to the 9th century. However, the most realistic theory would seem to indicate that the major events of this era, both inland and along the East African coasts, were connected with the long and complicated process of Bantu expansion mentioned in earlier chapters.

There are Arab, Persian, Indonesian, and Chinese documents dating back to this period that also indicate the existence of a busy black slave trade all along the Indian Ocean coastline. Ivory was also exported, and from the 10th century onward gold was the major export from the Zambezi region. Cotton cloth and luxury goods, like rich textiles, china, and porcelain were imported.

It is important to remember that the Persian Gulf region was also connected to Europe and the Far East. This explains the Chinese porcelain found during archeological digs in the rich East African coastal cities.

Merchants and Sunnite Arab refugees founded the Somalian cities of Brava and Mogadishu, probably during the 10th century. The most important Islamic expansion, however, took place in the 13th century, with the colonization of the whole coastline as far as the island of Sofala by a dominant group of Arabs—the Shirazi. Their most important settlement was in Kilwa, which became the most important center for the gold trade in the 14th century. All the groups of islands in the Indian Ocean, including the large island of Madagascar, became part of the oceanic trade network in this period.

Map showing the East African coast from Kenya to the northern region of Mozambique, together with the largest lakes

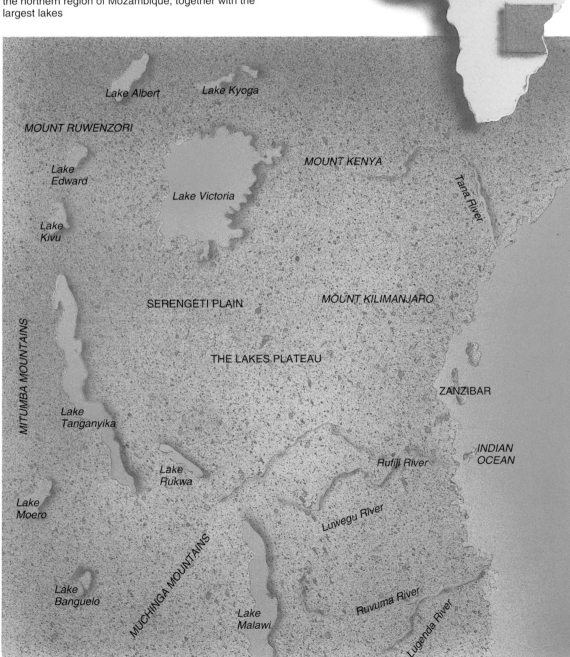

Carved wooden door made by the Mdaburu people

Arabic inscription carved into red brick

Market scene: people crowd into the narrow streets of the souk, a typical quarter of a Muslim city; food is sold in open-air stalls, and people of different social and ethnic origins mingle in front of the entrance to a mosque and other important buildings.

Beautiful silver jewelry from Mombasa, measuring 2 3/8 inches in diameter

THE BIRTH OF THE SWAHILI CIVILIZATION

The term "Swahili" comes from Arabic and means peoples of the coast (sahel—coast). The original Swahili people stretched from Mogadishu in today's Somalia to Sofala in Mozambique. The language comes in large part from Bantu but contains loan words from Arabic, Persian, Gujarati, Turkish, Portuguese, and even English. The Swahili people developed as a result of contacts between the Africans who lived near the coast and the Indian Ocean merchants with whom they traded, probably before the first century A.D.

An example of how new ethnic groups form and how languages merge can be found in the Swahili and the Hausa, who are located in northern Nigeria. Both languages—Swahili and Hausa—were formed from the mergers of trading cultures. And the formation of what came to be called Swahili and Hausa peoples also resulted from intermarriages between groups of traders who came together and lived in city-states, such as Katsina in Nigeria and Mombasa in Kenya. Today Swahili is the official language of both Kenya and Tanzania, although it is widely spoken in parts of central Africa as well as in coastal Somalia and down to northern Mozambique.

Archeologist Mark Horton worked in Shanga, a small community on an island located off the northern Kenya coast. Horton found that Islam had come to Shanga by the 9th century, that the local people had a king, and that Indians as well as traders from Arabia came and stayed during the winter monsoon which blew them in from the east. Africans from the interior came to the islands where they conducted "trade fairs" with the Indian Ocean traders, and when the monsoon winds blew from the north, the Africans retreated to their dwellings inland and the traders returned home.

Horton's findings indicate that the local Africans were also sailing up and down the East African coast where they conducted trade independent of the outsiders. The local building in stone, coral, and lime probably originated in the Red Sea areas and was carried south by the African traders who eventually moved from only part-time occupancy on these coastal islands to permanent residences there.

In time Swahili caravans spread as far west as Uganda and into central Africa, where they were heavily involved in obtaining slaves for shipment to Arabia, India, Persia, and elsewhere in the east. In this capacity they continued their role as middlemen between the Africans and the Indian Ocean traders.

Islam was the religion practiced by all the traders in these coastal trading city-states, with the exception of the Hindu merchants who may have been among the earliest traders of all. As these Swahili communities grew and prospered, locals became landowners of some significance, and with the spread of an agricultural economy, slavery increased. This was especially true on the Kenyan coast and in Zanzibar.

The Muslim hold over trade in the Indian Ocean was broken at the end of the 15th century by the arrival of the Portuguese. They hoped to take over control of the gold trade they had heard so much about and so desperately needed.

In 1505 the Portuguese took possession of Sofala and Kilwa. They then made repeated attempts to reach the inland regions by installing trading posts and building forts along the course of the Zambezi River. They sacked the main Swahili cities, forcing them to pay such high tributes, or taxes, that these areas became bankrupt and fell into decline. In 1593 the Portuguese founded Fort Jesus, near Mombasa, to protect themselves from Turkish invasions. The Portuguese never managed to dominate the area totally but they did keep some control

A reconstruction of the Great Mosque in Kilwa. The work was probably completed in the 15th century.

for about a century. Toward the end of this time their influence was systematically reduced, mainly by the appearance of other European rivals in the region. However, the economic and cultural decline the Portuguese had caused in the region proved permanent. During the 16th century, however, some Swahili cities experienced a period of revival and more routes to the inland areas of East Africa were opened. This helped to spread the Swahili language, which is the most widely spoken language in the East African region today.

Facade and tower of the Fort of Kilwa, an island off the coast of Tanzania, with a typical ship sailing near the coast

Illustration of a ship from a 13th-century Arab manuscript. The picture is an indication of the presence of Africans on board ships using trade routes across the Indian Ocean.

Chinese porcelain plate built into the walls of the mosque at Juma, for decoration

A tomb made from pillars in Mabrui; notice the decoration of inset Chinese porcelain plates.

MADAGASCAR

Madagascar, also known as the Great or Red Island, is situated in the Indian Ocean. It is twice as long as Florida and is separated from the African coast by the Mozambique Channel, about 248 miles wide at its narrowest point. In total area Madagascar is 226,657 square miles and is one of the most densely populated countries that can be considered part of Africa.

According to geologists Madagascar was originally part of an ancient continent called Gondwana, which has since disappeared. Its origins probably gave Madagascar the role of "bridge" between Asia and Africa, which it still fills. This description is particularly true when we examine the animals living on the island today. The unusual mixture of species makes Madagascar rather like a mysterious Noah's Ark. Interestingly none of the species of large African carnivores are present, but there are numerous members of the lemur family, chameleons, snakes, tortoises, birds, butterflies, and tens of thousands of invertebrates. Recent research has found that in the past, animals from as far away as Australia, New Zealand, and Indonesia were present on the island.

A few of these species are still present on Madagascar today. The species of Indonesian origin arrived with the Indonesians who were the first people to colonize the island.

Madagascar is rather like a "hyphen" between two continents. This characteristic is also reflected in the ethnic make-up of its people. They are a Malaysian-Polynesian mixture, very different from the peoples of southern Africa, even though the latter also contributed to the ethnic mix of the island.

Many aspects of Madagascar's ancient history remain a mystery to us, due to the lack of archeological and oral sources. We have only scant evidence from written Arab sources dating back to the first thousand years A.D. Unfortunately these sources are rather difficult to interpret clearly. However, with our present knowledge it would seem the island of Madagascar was the scene of successive waves of Indonesian colonization, probably sometime during the first five centuries A.D. This period of colonization lasted until about the 13th century. The Indonesian peoples gradually mixed with other peoples, believed by some experts to have been the Bantu, who originally came from the African coasts. The east coastal region of Madagascar was the first to be colonized, followed later by population of the inland region.

Some historians claim that contacts between the Indonesian and original Bantu peoples allowed plants like coconuts and bananas to be introduced to the African continent. These plants were the main reason for the Bantu farmers' agricultural advance over the Khoisan peoples who were hunters and gatherers. The same contacts also led to the introduction of millet and beans for cultivation on the island of Madagascar.

The first trading connections with the Arabs began only in the 11th century. This was probably because Madagascar offered neither gold nor ivory to attract the merchants from the east. Contacts intensified after the 13th century due to the Sultan of Kilwa's influence over the Comoros and Mascarene archipelagoes. There was no political conquest nor the foundation of great commercial centers like those along the African coasts, however. Fresh groups of immigrants arrived and mixed with the peoples already living on the island. Eighteen ethnic groups are present on the island today, living together in a unique cultural melting pot.

The Europeans discovered the island of Madagascar in 1500. Captain Diogo Dias named it St. Lorenzo's Isle, but it was only a century later that the Portuguese, followed by the French, attempted to colonize. The Portuguese constructed a fort in the Diego Suarez Bay to the north, while the French built Fort Dolphin in the southeast.

At the end of the 17th century, Madagascar was the site of a rather strange experiment—the foundation of the Republic of Libertalia. This was a new base built by English and French pirates who had

Wooden granary of the Zafimaniry people

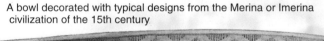
A bowl decorated with typical designs from the Merina or Imerina civilization of the 15th century

A paddy field on irrigated terraces, near a small village of sundried straw and mud huts from the central plateau region of Madagascar. This type of farming and village is typical of the Merina peoples, an ethnic group of Indonesian origin and traditions.

been chased away from the Caribbean area. The last pirate was eliminated in 1730.

Meanwhile small "kingdoms" had sprung up on Madagascar, probably modeled on the Arab sultanates thriving along the African coast. They often fought among themselves for control of the traffic and trade with the island's inland regions. The principal commercial activity was the slave trade. With the introduction of firearms, the struggle for supremacy and more territory became fiercer. At the end of the 18th century, the Kingdom of Merina became the most powerful on the island. It gained prestige under a king with an extremely long name—Andrianampoinimerina. The rise of the Kingdom of Merina largely depended on his taking part in a treaty promising a supply of slaves in return for firearms. Those weapons helped him extend his control over the entire central plateau region of Madagascar around 1810.

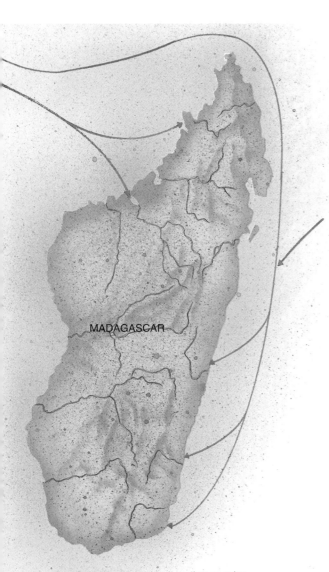

MADAGASCAR

A lemur. The long-tailed lemurs are among the most interesting mammals for scientists to study in Madagascar. Zoologically speaking they almost completely span the history of evolution. They are the most primitive expression of the order of primates. The size of a cat, with a long muzzle and tail, they live in large groups that move from tree to tree, feeding on fruit and leaves.

The map shows the two main sources of the island's population—Indonesians who arrived on the island between the 12th and 13th centuries mixed with the African population, later followed by Arabs and African converts to Islam.

▰ Routes of Bantu and Indonesian peoples
▰ Routes of peoples converted to Islam

A fossilized egg from one of the largest birds that ever existed. It became extinct because it was hunted by the first inhabitants of Madagascar. This bird was about ten feet tall and resembled an ostrich. It laid giant eggs, fragments of which may still be found in river silt deposits on the southern portion of the island. The egg in the drawing is compared with a hen's egg.

Group of Lukeni men watching the first arrival of Portuguese ships

Dwarf Ovancilliaria shell, used as money in the ancient kingdom of the Congo

Square-sailed Portuguese caravel surrounded by native dugout canoes. In the background, hills covered with lush vegetation.

Wooden sculpture from the Suku group (Kwango region, Zaire)

The illustration (left) attempts to show the Portuguese effect on the ancient kingdom of the Congo from an African rather than a European point of view. The artist has tried to convey the feeling of amazement these native people must have experienced at the arrival of the huge, square-sailed ships. The lush vegetation of the region and the physical prowess of the people are also illustrated. The shell is the dwarf Ovancilliaria shell used locally as money. The same shells were used as money in the first exchanges between the Portuguese and the Congolese.

THE ARRIVAL OF THE EUROPEANS

Portuguese Voyages of Discovery

1418	Madeira
1434	Canaries and Cape Bojador
1439	Azores
1441–44	Cape Blanc and Cape Verde Island
1460	Cape Verde and the mouth of the Senegal River
1471	Elmina (fort built in 1482)
1482	Congo River estuary
1487–88	Expedition led by Bartolomeo Dias around Cape of Good Hope
1497–99	Expedition led by Vasco da Gama and discovery of the route to India

The 14th and 15th centuries witnessed a major turning point in the history of the Mediterranean region. Despite the breakup of unity caused by the spread of Islam and the tensions created by the Christian Crusades, the Mediterranean had remained the absolute center of seagoing trade. The power of the Italian maritime republics had increased, particularly that of Venice. The importance achieved by Venice drove the newer nations in the Iberian Peninsula, Spain and Portugal, to begin the search for fresh trade routes outside the Mediterranean, in the Atlantic Ocean. It is important to remember that both Spain and Portugal were already involved in the struggle against Islam in their own countries at this time.

The first to begin the search was the Portuguese prince, Henry the Navigator, at the start of the 15th century. Aboard their huge, square-sailed ships and with the aid of increasingly sophisticated navigation charts and the newly developed system of tacking against the winds, his captains discovered the Canary Islands. Later they landed in Madeira, which had already been reached by an Italian ship a century earlier. Henry's men explored the Azores and sailed as far as the mouth of the Senegal River, believing it to be the western mouth of the Nile River. Toward the middle of the century they reached the Cape Verde Islands and, in 1482, landed at the mouth of the Congo River. During this early stage of exploration their chief contacts were with Benin on the West African coast and the Congo.

After the death of Henry the Navigator, his mission was continued by another Portuguese prince, John II. In 1486 he commissioned Bartolomeo Dias to explore all of the West African coast as far as its extreme southern limits. The voyage was only partially successful as Dias went beyond the Cape without realizing it. He understood on the way back, and called it "The Cape of Storms." It was John II who changed the name to "The Cape of Good Hope." However, Dias's voyage of discovery had proved that a sea route to India really did exist. Several years later Vasco da Gama was commissioned to establish the best route and open the first commercial contacts with the East. A brief but highly prosperous period began for the Portuguese. They were accompanied and eventually replaced by ships and merchants from all of the European powers.

The main reason for the Portuguese explorations was the search for trade openings with the Orient and access to its wealth. Interest in the African continent itself was slight at the beginning, but the navigators and merchants, in their reports, often praised the organization and civilization of the peoples with whom they had the most contact. We shall return to this subject more fully later. However, during this early stage some gold and ivory were traded until a much greater interest grew in the slave trade.

Together with economic and trade interests in the African continent, conversion to Christianity became another Portuguese objective. This included an alliance with a legendary kingdom of priests supposedly existing somewhere in East Africa. This was part of their plan to make possible an attack on the Turkish powers from another direction. This objective failed, and the Portuguese only succeeded in creating limited settlements along the African coasts. Later their colonial empire was built using these original settlements as a basis.

One of the few positive results of the Portuguese presence in Africa along the Atlantic coast was the introduction of food crops brought from South America such as corn and cassava, or manioc. This created a kind of revolution in food production and led to a massive increase in population.

Group of Lukeni merchants and hunters armed with shields and lances
Painted, wooden mask (inset) crafted by the Teke or Tsaye peoples (Congo)

THE ORIGIN AND FORMATION OF THE KINGDOM OF THE CONGO

Before we discuss the Kingdom of Congo, we must unravel some of the complexities that characterized earlier societies in central Africa. We are indebted to the oral traditions and to the pioneering fieldwork of historian Jan Vansina for information on the early Luba and Lunda kingdoms which had developed by the 14th and 15th centuries. Luba, the earliest of these kingdoms to emerge, was near the southeastern border of the dense Zaire forest, and Lunda was located about 125 miles east of the bend in the Kasai River. At an early date the Luba people benefited from iron imports brought in through trade, and later copper from the Zambia/Zaire area to the east. Thus the Luba and other peoples in this vast area of central Africa developed

an artistic tradition as well as sophisticated agricultural and fishing tools and techniques.

By about 1300 a group of Luba had organized into a political kingdom, with the leaders claiming to have mystical powers that enabled them to stay in office. According to the Luba, the first dynasty was founded by a man who came from the Songye people in the north. This leader was soon overthrown by another, Ilunga Kalala, who in oral traditions was said to be a great hunter possessing magical powers. Because of his supposed supernatural powers, Ilunga Kalala and his descendants were able to rule the Luba, and later to extend their rule over other nearby groups, including eventually the Lunda people.

Around mid-15th century, a discontented member of Luba royalty moved in among the Lunda, who had no centralized kingdom. He was said to have been handsome in addition to the magical powers he claimed, and thus was attractive to a Lunda queen whom he married and with whom he began a new dynasty. The Lunda did not have the same developed technology that the Luba had, but the Luba who came in brought their metal working skills. The Luba royalty also respected the local Lunda spirits who were mainly connected with the land, since the Lunda were primarily farmers. In addition, they kept the loyalty of the Lunda by placing their leaders in positions of importance in the royal court.

Wooden ceremonial seat carved in the form of a kneeling human figure bearing offerings.
Hemba people (Zaire)
View of the Congolese region

Discord, however, developed among the Lunda leaders as it had done earlier with the Luba. Rival royalty moved away and founded other dynasties among the ethnic groups to the south and west. These included the Lozi and the Luena.

Among the Mbundu people farther south in present-day Angola, notions of a monarchy developed along lines similar to those of the Luba and the Lunda. The Mbundu, the Luba, and Lunda were all Bantu speakers, although because of separate development over a long period of time their languages differed significantly. It is possible that the Luba may have spread as far as the Ndongo, a sub-

group of the Mbundu. They developed similar skills in metalworking and claimed magical powers which helped to unify the state under a single ruler.

Farther south also in today's Angola, were the Ovimbundo and Ovambo people about whose early culture we know very little. By the 15th century, they were farmers and had developed a sense of separate identity.

The most important kingdom to arise in this area was Congo. The people were originally farmers but because of the savanna land they occupied, and the iron tools they could use, they produced surplus foodstuffs which they could

then trade for copper and other luxury items. By the early 14th century, the Congo villages ran from the Atlantic coast below Malebo Pool to near the Kwango River in the east, and down to border the Ndongo in Angola. They were ideally situated to engage in trade, with water supplying part of their border, and they were able to develop skills as fishermen. A single kingdom developed by the 15th century, and the king was called *manikongo*. It was these Congo peoples with whom the Portuguese first developed trade. The Portuguese later sent missionaries to convert the kingdom to Christianity.

EFFORTS TO MAKE THE CONGO CHRISTIAN AND THE FOUNDING OF ANGOLA

In 1482, when Diego Cao of Portugal, first reached the mouth of the Congo River, he very quickly learned about the Kingdom of the Congo. He sent a diplomatic mission to visit the king, the manikongo. During his next voyage he visited the capital of the Congo in person. On his return to Portugal, he gave a full account of the organization and wealth of the kingdom. He explained how the king was at the head of a vast circle of regional rulers, called *mani,* or lords. They in turn were

responsible for the control of the villages together with the traditional village chiefs. It appeared the state had also organized a regular system of taxation.

In this first stage of contacts between the Portuguese and African groups one of the chief Portuguese objective was to convert the African peoples to Christianity. The Portuguese approach was therefore planned with this aim especially in mind.

In 1489 the manikongo sent a diplomatic mission to Lisbon, the capital of Portugal. A year later

missionaries arrived in the Congo to instruct the sovereign and his court in the Roman Catholic faith. The missionaries were accompanied by bricklayers, carpenters, and every type of craftsman, who began rebuilding the royal palaces and the most important buildings in the capital in stone.

The manikongo was converted to Christianity in 1491 and attempted to carry out the conversion of his people. The people were violently opposed to this process. When the sovereign died in 1507, he

Primitive arrowheads

Group of Lukeni hunters armed with bows and arrows

Map of the ancient region of the Congo now called Zaire

Zaire River

ANCIENT REGION OF THE CONGO (ZAIRE)

Cuango River

Cuanza River

Woman in the fields carrying a large basket to collect fruit and roots

Banana plants probably introduced in the region after contacts with the peoples of Madagascar. Notice the roofs and smoke from fires in the village just below the plateau area.

was succeeded by his son, who had been christened with the name of Alfonso. He continued the program of converting the people to Christianity, ordering destruction of pagan idols. He also changed the name of his capital city to San Salvador. Even before becoming king, Alfonso had sent one of his sons, Don Enrico, to Lisbon with a group of other young nobles. Don Enrico was ordained as a priest in 1518, and despite his young age he was nominated bishop to the Congo. But his work had little success, and in 1543 his father died.

The final years of Alfonso's reign had been marred by the behavior of the Portuguese. Now they only seemed interested in enriching themselves through the newly introduced slave trade, neglecting any other objective. Alfonso had even tried to send a protest to the pope in Rome, asking for his intervention, but to no avail.

Directly to the south of the Congo was the region later called Angola, home of the Ovimbundu and Ovambo. There the Portuguese tried to seize slaves directly. From 1575 on, they attempted to found a colony. There were three phases to this process. First, the Portuguese tried to locate and exploit the rich mineral deposits supposedly present in the region. They proved to be nonexistent. During the second phase, they concentrated on the search for slaves. A series of military raids was carried out in the interior with the aim of taking prisoners, but this also proved to be extremely difficult. Finally they decided to try and rebuild a native kingdom, to have a trading partner that would organize the raids for them. Even this attempt was a partial failure. However, the Portuguese demand for slaves had important effects on the interior of the region.

At the same time, the Portuguese were forced to deal with strong and growing competition from the Dutch, French, and English all along the Atlantic coastline of Africa. This competition furthered the interests of several African states situated farther inland, far enough to be out of the reach of the Portuguese military expeditions. This allowed them to impose their own conditions on the slave trade, which continued with increasing intensity all along the coast.

THE CONGO MONARCHY

In the Kingdom of the Congo, and in all Bantu kingdoms in general, the power was in the hands of the king, helped by a suitable number of court dignitaries. The king was expected to be handsome, have excellent personal qualities, and look extremely healthy. Copper and ivory were the materials used as royal symbols. The king sat on a finely inlaid stool while his dignitaries sat on the floor. The king held a scepter of power. Members of the ruling classes were given special clothing, such as skirts made from feathers, animals skins, and finely embroidered hats. The illustration on page 51 shows a meeting of the king's council.

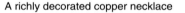
A richly decorated copper necklace

These pages will be dedicated to a fairly detailed description of the type of nation the Portuguese found in the Kingdom of the Congo. There are two reasons for this choice of nation: because of the amount of information available on the subject, and because this model, with few variations, was typical of all the nations in sub-Saharan Africa. This included the area from the Sudan to the tiny kingdoms in the region of the great lakes of eastern Africa and as far as Zimbabwe Monomotapa in southern Africa.

The nation revolved around the central figure of the king, who was held to be "divine" or god-like, or at the very least, felt to have a special charm or popular appeal. Some believe this concept of the ruler had derived from the figure of the pharoah in ancient Egypt. Others think the concept was linked to the progressive spread of an agriculturally based economy together with special skills in the forging of metals, especially iron.

The king, manikongo, had power over the government. He was believed to have divine powers and was honored as if he were a god. If he were not himself a god, then he was believed to have descended from the gods or from the ancestor who had founded the community. His people believed him to be able to communicate with the spirits of the ancestors and the spirits of the earth and water and to have the power to please the forces of nature better than anyone else. People believed that the fertility of their land was linked to the physical well-being of the king. In the name of the gods, the king controlled the use of the land on which the sur-

vival of his people depended. He decided when to sow and when to harvest. His funeral rites often involved human sacrifice and his successor was believed to be the reincarnation of the king. The king lived apart from the common people and was not to be seen while carrying out ordinary actions like eating and drinking. He communicated to others through a spokesman and gave audience while hidden behind a curtain.

His court was elaborate and luxurious. He received ambassadors from Portugal sitting on a special, square-shaped ivory stool. He wore a finely embroidered hat and several bracelets on his wrists, and he held a bag symbolizing his absolute power to demand taxes. The sovereign's wealth was assured by his monopoly over the currency—cowry shells—small shells that come from the island of Luanda.

The king's wife was the female head of the royal family. Although the king had absolute power, there were some limitations. The succession to the throne had to be sanctioned by a sort of election. A member of the royal family was elected by the elders and dignitaries of the court. Regional rulers were nominated by the king, but his choice was limited to certain eligible families. The king was advised by a special King's Council made up of ten to twelve members.

A special bodyguard was directly employed by the king, together with a small number of permanent soldiers. In wartime he enrolled soldiers sent by the regional rulers he nominated.

Portuguese accounts have left us vivid descriptions of the responsibilities of the major court dignitaries, but we need to remember that their understanding was probably limited to recognizing the positions and duties similar to those existing in Europe.

It would seem that even though the Bantu kingdoms were well organized, many were politically unstable. This was perhaps because they lacked procedures for the process of succession to the throne and because it was extremely difficult to guarantee constant loyalty from the outlying peoples and clans toward the center of power.

A royal tent (sometimes covered with raffia mats), where the King's Council met. Here the king is seated on an inlaid stool and is holding a symbol of power, decorated with a female figure—symbolic of fertility. Other dignitaries are seated on the ground.

51

THE AFRICAN ECONOMY

The illustration below shows a marketplace in Mbanza, the Congo capital, before (left) and after (right) the arrival of the Europeans. The typical goods on sale before the Europeans came mostly from the land—livestock, salt, handicrafts made from ivory, wood, and copper, as well as handwoven raffia mats. Only court officials were allowed to sell the mats, which represented a kind of official money. After the arrival of the Portuguese, the market continued for some time as it had in the past, but the variety of goods was quickly reduced when the slave trade took over as the major trading activity.

As already stated, the economy of all the Bantu states was based on agriculture, raising livestock, and processing iron. Their system of agriculture was founded on an extremely long cycle of crop rotation. The crops were grown on areas of land reclaimed from the forests by burning down the trees. Livestock was raised in regions where it was possible to graze the animals. The Bantu often lived in or near forests which provided the necessary fuel to feed the blacksmiths' fires for smelting and processing iron. This is how the Bantu developed better weapons. During the period of Bantu expansion, these superior weapons helped them to impose themselves on the existing populations where they decided to settle, particularly in southern Africa. The local people depended on hunting and gathering fruit and roots.

All the historical sources—archeological, oral, European, and Arab—dating back to the end of the 15th century confirm the existence of numerous Bantu states. They were located mainly in the region of the great lakes of eastern Africa and on the plateaus of central and southern Africa, but we shall not be able to study them all in this text.

Instead, let us take the Bantu Kingdom of the Congo as an example. It is one of the Bantu kingdoms about which we have the most information. We have seen something about its origin. It seemed extremely rich to the Portuguese explorers when they arrived. According to Portuguese sources, their arrival at the Bantu king's court was greeted by a huge crowd of thousands. The Portuguese were especially impressed by the Bantu aristocrats, who were dressed in their fabulous costumes and armed with buffalo hide shields and iron swords, and by the bows and arrows of the king's soldiers.

(above) A finely carved elephant tusk

(below left) A court official weaving a raffia mat on a loom. Only court officials had the right to do this work since the mats were also used as money.

(right) Women carrying goods to market

The Europeans found a flourishing internal market where products from the land and objects like raffia mats, made by artisans, were exchanged. The raffia mats were considered a form of official money, like the cowry shells, and the court officials held the monopoly on their production. The craftsmanship was dissimilar to that of the Ife civilization and the artisans of the Kingdom of Benin; instead it showed that the Bantu craftsmen were masters at the art of wood carving.

The Portuguese entered the Bantu market easily. They organized trade caravans in the immediate inland regions, which were led initially by Portuguese merchants, later by half-castes and sometimes even by slaves. The Portuguese invented the name *pombeiros* for the slaves who agreed to do this work. In exchange for salt and European goods these caravans acquired ivory, copper, raffia mats and, very soon, slaves. As in other areas along the Atlantic coast of Africa, as the slave trade became stronger all the other forms of trade weakened and finally ceased altogether. The existence of organized markets and accepted currency such as the cowry shells in the Congo and the raffia mats in Luango was unquestionable proof of the level of development reached by these peoples before the Europeans arrived.

In other West African coastal regions, trade between Africans and Europeans was organized in various ways. We are not sure exactly how the early Portuguese traders dealt with the Africans before they developed a pidgin language through which they could communicate. Evidently it could be depicted as what has been called "silent trade," a term that conveyed the impression that each group simply placed their goods in the open for inspection, then retreated a few paces away for the opposite side to place their items of trade alongside, weighing what they would barter in exchange for what was offered. This implied a sort of trust that is uncommon, especially to traders. No doubt a great deal of gesturing and movement of goods back and forth took place, but not without the active presence of merchants on both sides.

Only a short time after the Portuguese arrival, slaves became the chief merchandise in the San Salvador market.

Ivory bracelets inlaid with lead

53

Camp of Khoisan hunters

Map of
Southern Africa

SOUTHERN AFRICA

Zambezi R.

Tete
Sena

Zimbabwe

Cape Colony

SOUTHERN AFRICA

From a historical viewpoint, southern Africa is still one of the lesser-known regions of the continent because of the lack of information and archeological remains available. The magnificent ruins of Great Zimbabwe are an exception. They were objects of wonder for a long time but were only recently recognized as being the remnants of the "royal village" of the Kingdom of Monomotapa. All the gold traded along the East African coast came from here. This kingdom was probably very similar to the Kingdom of the Congo. Other smaller kingdoms existed nearby. Some were founded by Bantu peoples during their expansion southward and others, perhaps already scarce in the 17th century, belonged to the Khoisan peoples (the San and Khoi). The Khoisan were limited to the southern Atlantic region and by the late 17th century were far less developed than the Bantu. In 1652 Fort Cape was established. This was the beginning of the future Cape Colony.

The type of state founded on the authority of a monarch revered almost like a god, typical of the Congo, was also present in the eastern region of southern Africa. The most famous is the Kingdom of Monomotapa Zimbabwe, situated in the region known from the late 1800s until 1980 as Rhodesia. After the country gained its independence in 1980, it retook the name Zimbabwe.

The stone enclosures that were known as "Great Zimbabwe" were constructed sometime in the 13th and 14th centuries. Bantu speakers had trickled east and south into southern Africa by this time, and they had branched off into separate ethnic groups

such as the Shona, the Zulu, and the Xhosa. The ancestors of today's modern Shona built the huge enclosure which served as the capital for the Shona state. Among the features of this stone enclosure was its location at the top of a hill, where the Shona could look into a valley below and see the arrival of possible enemies. Beyond that it was unique in that no mortar was used in its construction, despite its height of more than 40 feet. Cattle-keeping was an important economic base for the early people of Zimbabwe and they had access to a large open area outside the stone walls in which their cattle could graze. Trade, too, was important. It was based on closeness to the Sabi River. Here the people could control the trade between the goldfields in the interior and the merchants on the coast of Sofala (in today's Mozambique). Interestingly, although the local merchants traded in gold, they preferred to wear jewelry fashioned from copper. They also traded in ivory, as did the Swahili farther north.

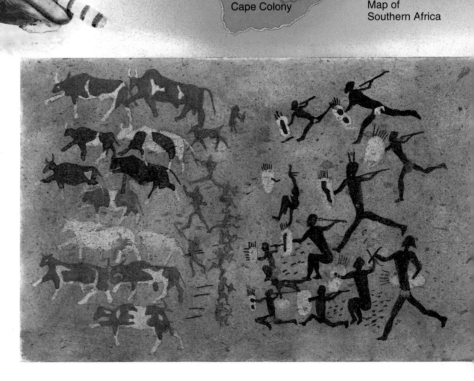

Khoisan cave paintings in the Kalahari Desert showing a battle between the Khoisan and the Bantu for the possession of a herd

Great Zimbabwe reconstruction surrounded by a Khoisan village.

In the mid-15th century Great Zimbabwe was deserted. There are several oral traditions that relate to why the Shona builders left. Some think that pastoral people from the outside conquered them and took over the area to graze their cattle. Others suggest that lack of salt caused the original occupants to move on. Still other traditions suggest that as the goldfields dried up, so did trade.

Nevertheless, the Portuguese were lured by stories of "the land of gold." They set out to find it by sailing up the Zambezi River from the river ports of Sena and Tete, which they had founded in 1531. In their reports the Portuguese changed the native name Mwenemutapa to Monomotapa. It would seem, however, that by this time the kingdom had already entered a period of decline, because the court had moved from the region of Great Zimbabwe to an inland region which has never really been identified.

Bantu shepherds with their herd

Carved stone monolith in the form of a bird; probably the symbol for the people of Great Zimbabwe of the spirits of their ancestors. This is the only monolith that remains in its original position.

Plan of Great Zimbabwe

In 1560 the first Roman Catholic missionaries arrived in Monomotapa, but the king decided to convert only in 1652. The Portuguese were really more interested in the gold than in religious conversion. They dominated the kingdom to a certain extent, but the trading system they had attempted to create in the Indian Ocean to substitute for the one organized by the Muslims never really took hold. It was undermined by small ships owned by Arab smugglers and by the Africans' refusal to buy goods from Portuguese merchants who held the trade monopoly. The Portuguese were further upset from the 17th and 18th centuries on by the growing competition from other European powers. The result of the Portuguese presence was the decline of the preexisting forms of African civilization in the area.

Another European settlement in southern Africa developed in a totally different way. This was the Dutch settlement in Table Bay, near the Cape of Good Hope. In 1652 a flotilla of the Dutch East India Company founded a supply station here for ships bound for the Indies. The settlement soon became a colony that was opposed by the Company but supported by the people they had sent to colonize. The colonists quickly came into conflict with the Khoisan peoples. The San were hunters and gatherers. The Khoisan were mainly cattle keepers. These peoples had been pushed west in southern Africa by the advance of the Bantu peoples. As a result of these conflicts, the numbers of Khoisan were drastically reduced, and only very few isolated groups remain today.

THE ATLANTIC SLAVE TRADE

The Atlantic slave trade did not introduce the practice of slavery to Africa. Slaves were already present within African society. Arab merchants had organized overland slave trading using the caravan routes across the Sahara and a similar type of maritime commerce across the Indian Ocean. The Atlantic slave trade did introduce new elements to the activity, however. Greater numbers of slaves were traded than ever before, and the traders' sole aim was to make a profit. Slaves became the most important "commodity," and the slave trade almost totally destroyed every other type of commerce between Africa and Europe.

Slavery was therefore present in Africa—as in most civilizations throughout history—well before the Atlantic slave trade began. The Arab slave trade continued to operate side by side with the Atlantic version. The slavery already present in Africa was much different from that practiced in the New World. Often when wars developed between neighboring people, the winners captured the losers and enslaved them rather than take the chance of having to fight them again. In that case, slaves were dispersed throughout the state. Some were placed in domestic positions, some in the army, and some became artisans. Because slaves had no families—extended kin—they were dependent on the people whom they served, yet they were often able to move up in status. In some societies, they married into the owning families and their children were free. In others, they could move up into high positions of administrations or become generals in the army.

During periods of drought or famine, chiefs frequently sold women and children into slavery in order for them to live. This is not to say that slavery in Africa was entirely kind and gentle. Masters and mistresses could be cruel to their slaves just as they could exercise harsh treatment over peasants or other low-status people. Much depended on personal behavior and attitudes, but there was no large-scale exploitation of human life such as that developed on some of the plantations in the West Indies and elsewhere across the Atlantic.

The fundamental differences introduced by the Atlantic slave trade were the increase in the numbers of slaves traded, the duration of the activity—which lasted at least three and a half centuries—and the strictly economic nature of the commerce. It really began with the introduction of sugarcane plantations which needed a plentiful supply of cheap labor for heavy repetitive work. Sugarcane was exported by the Asian countries into the Mediterranean region between the 11th and 13th centuries. Plantations were also set up in North Africa. When the Europeans began to explore the Atlantic coasts of Africa sugarcane plantations were introduced into the Canary Islands and to the Cape Verde Islands. The next step was to take sugarcane plantations to the newly conquered American colonies; to Santo Domingo in 1493, just a year after Columbus's first voyage, and into Brazil in 1550. In this way the spread of

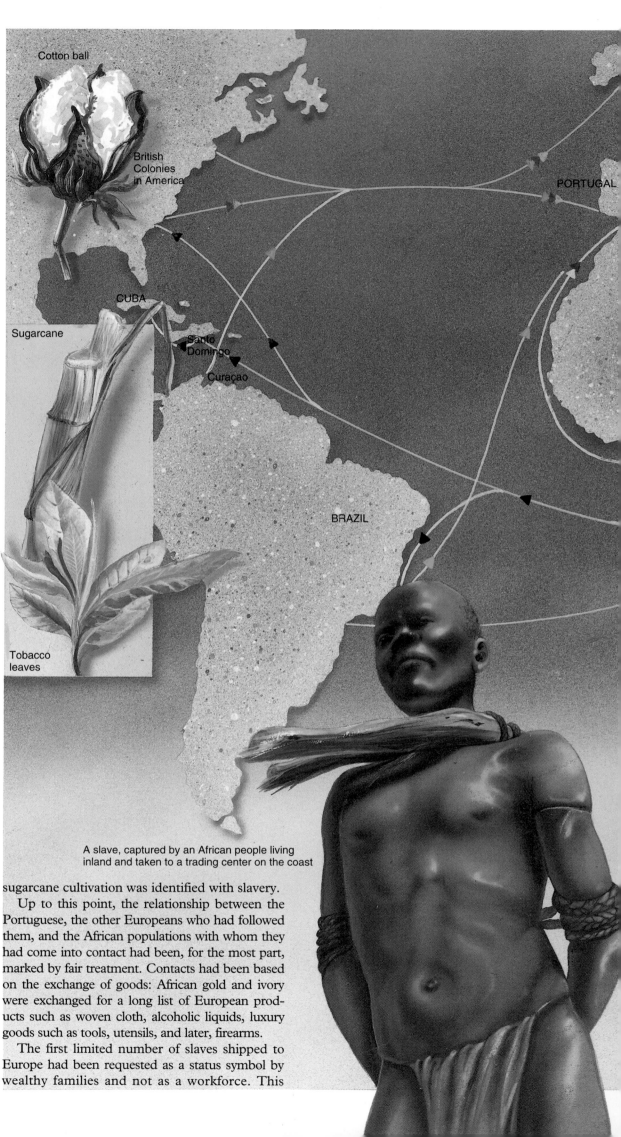

A slave, captured by an African people living inland and taken to a trading center on the coast

sugarcane cultivation was identified with slavery.

Up to this point, the relationship between the Portuguese, the other Europeans who had followed them, and the African populations with whom they had come into contact had been, for the most part, marked by fair treatment. Contacts had been based on the exchange of goods: African gold and ivory were exchanged for a long list of European products such as woven cloth, alcoholic liquids, luxury goods such as tools, utensils, and later, firearms.

The first limited number of slaves shipped to Europe had been requested as a status symbol by wealthy families and not as a workforce. This

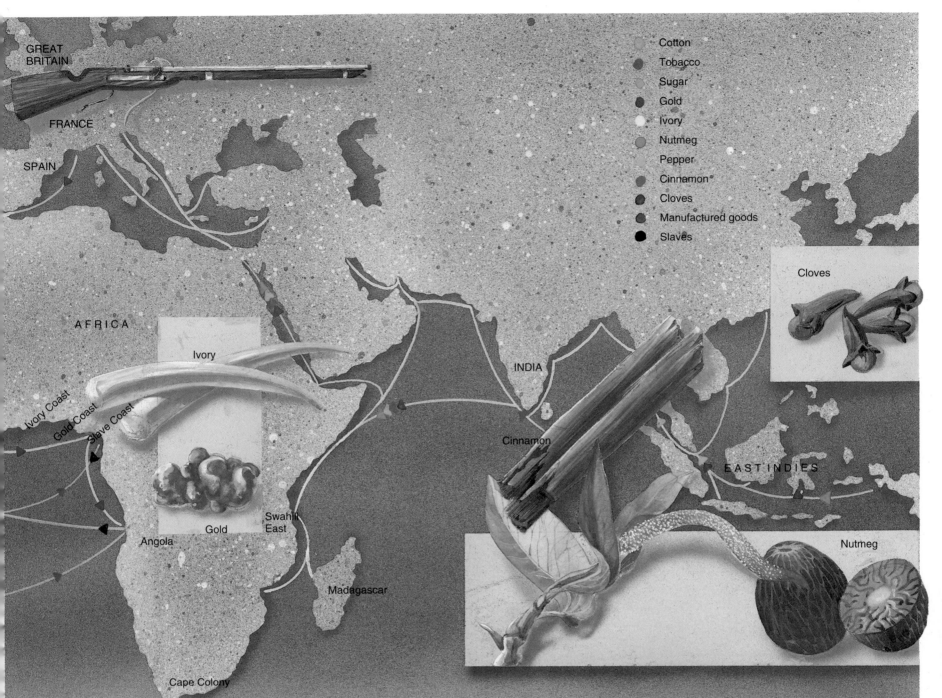

Cotton
Tobacco
Sugar
Gold
Ivory
Nutmeg
Pepper
Cinnamon
Cloves
Manufactured goods
Slaves

GREAT BRITAIN

FRANCE

SPAIN

AFRICA

Ivory

Ivory Coast

Gold Coast

Slave Coast

Gold

Angola

Swahili East

Madagascar

Cape Colony

INDIA

Cinnamon

EAST INDIES

Cloves

Nutmeg

The map shows the Atlantic slave trade routes between European countries, the coasts of West Africa, and the American colonies, where the slaves were chiefly used on plantations.

situation was completely changed by the fierce competition between the Spanish and the Portuguese during the period of colonial conquest immediately after the discovery of the New World. The colonists needed a strong workforce to exploit the mineral wealth and work the plantations in the new colonies. This need could not be satisfied by the scarce Native American populations whose numbers were rapidly reduced by illness and overwork, or by employing deported convicts, workers for hire, or temporary workers from their own societies. Those in the last three groups were needed in Europe to fight the wars that broke out continuously as power struggles between European nations continued.

The Spanish were the first to import slaves to work in their possessions in Mexico and Peru.

However, the Spanish took only a very limited part in the slave trade. During the 17th century the major demand came from the Portuguese colonies in America and from the Caribbean. The Atlantic slave trade reached mammoth proportions during the 18th century, when the Spanish and Portuguese empires were in decline and when the French, English, and Dutch had colonized the West Indies. At the same time, the demand for sugar in the European countries continued to increase.

The introduction of slavery to the British colonial cotton plantations in North America came much later. The first shipload of slaves arrived in 1619, but the slave traffic reached its height in the 18th century and even after being ruled illegal, continued in secret for a large part of the 19th century, too.

EUROPEAN FORTS IN AFRICA

Most important European forts on the Gold Coast (present-day Ghana) and along the Slave Coast (north of the Niger River, present-day Nigeria) (from west to east): the dates indicate when each fort was built and when it was taken over by another European group.

Axim (1503 Portuguese; Dutch from 1642)
Dixcove (1691 English)
Shama (1471 Portuguese; 1640 Dutch)
Elmina (1471 Portuguese; 1637 Dutch)
Cape Coast (1664 English)
Moree (1598 Dutch)
Fort James Accra (1673 English)
Christiansborg (1657 Swedish-Danish; 1850 English)

EFFECTS OF THE SLAVE TRADE ON AFRICAN REGIONS

Fon art, by the Dahomey (now Benin) people. Cotton war tunic with embroidered decorations. At the Paris, Musée de l'Homme

Africa paid a high price as a result of the slave trade. Depopulation was only relatively important if considered over the period of three and a half centuries, which is the time the commerce in slaves lasted. But the major damage to African society was the corruption caused by the slave trade. African society began to be structured exclusively around the slave trade, which robbed it of the ability to renew itself and to progress. This was the real price Africa had to pay for this period in its history, and the direct result was its loss of independence in the period that followed.

Much is known about the Africans who became slaves. Their story is part of the history of the Americas, their destination after forced emigration from the continent of their birth. Here we examine the events in Africa during and after the period of the trade.

The most recent research fixes the number of slaves taken from Africa during the period of the slave trade as fewer than 12 million. This figure is actually lower than previous estimates but does not include the number of people who died during the journey because of the terrible conditions on board ship. Some historians have estimated that as many as 20 to 25 percent of the slaves purchased in Africa died before reaching their destination. Others put the figure at 15 to 20 percent. In addition, although most historians accept that fewer than 12 million departed Africa in the Atlantic trade, that figure is still controversial, and several historians believe the number is much higher. We shall never know exactly how many African people left the continent in the trade, including those who were sent north across the Sahara Desert and those who were shipped across the Indian Ocean, where the trade lasted much longer. In all cases, the numbers would have to include those who died in the warfare that resulted in taking the captives, and those who died before they even reached a shipping port.

African rulers along the Atlantic coastline were especially active in the slave trade. Here the commerce reached its height, and part of the Gulf of Benin was even named the Slave Coast. Using firearms obtained in trade exchanges with the European merchants, these African rulers organized raids against the populations living farther inland to capture people they would then sell as slaves on the coast. There was a wide range of products offered by the Europeans during trade exchanges, such as alcoholic liquids, cloth, tools, luxury items, and perhaps even tobacco.

During the 17th and 18th centuries, a nation like Dahomey (now called Benin) became quite strong through its activities as a trading partner with the European merchants. The king of

Dahomey himself managed the trade directly. He formed a special bodyguard made up of only women to defend his position as absolute monarch. This famous group of about 5,000 women was nicknamed the "Amazons of Dahomey" by the Europeans.

The most serious result of the Atlantic slave trade was the halted development of the African nations. This included both those nations along the coast that built their power on this new trade, and those farther inland who were raided for slaves. Every form of progress was stopped. Politically and socially disruptive forces were set in motion. The new organization was centered around slavery. The two exceptions were the Portuguese colony of Angola and the Cape Colony founded by the Dutch. As explained earlier, the Portuguese presence in Angola resulted in total failure. The Cape Colony, founded as a supply post for ships en route to India, imported slaves from Madagascar and Malaysia on becoming a colony, but none were exported.

With very few exceptions, the previous forms of trade with the Europeans ceased. From the start of the slave trade, Europeans began to concentrate all their efforts in this direction and made no further attempts to penetrate deeper inside the continent. They left the job of capturing slaves, through raids inland, exclusively to their African partners. Even local crafts suffered competition from the items traded by the Europeans, and their production declined.

Perhaps the most negative result of the slave trade was the attitude of contempt toward the African peoples that spread across Europe and America. This attitude had not been present during the first contacts between Europeans and Africans, as the reports written by the first navigators and merchants make clear. In many ways this was the basis for the colonialism that followed in the 19th century. But that is another story.

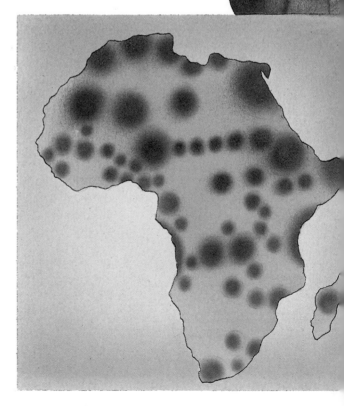

Altar figure made from sheets of hammered brass. This figure is almost lifesize and represents Gu, the god of war. It probably comes from the palace of Behenzin, a king of Dahomey

This map shows the African area most affected by raids for the purpose of capturing slaves

Women's army founded by a Dahomey king to
act as his bodyguard. The picture was inspired by
a sketch drawn by a contemporary European explorer.

59

The illustrations on pages 60–61 suggest the complex system of trade and cultural relations existing in Africa from the 7th to the 11th centuries (page 60) and from the 12th to the 18th centuries (page 61). The same setting has been used on both pages to illustrate each period to help emphasize the changes.

Main Goods Traded and Regions of Origin

Gold: Deposits in West Africa—Shaba (Zaire) and Northern Zambia; Zimbabwe
Copper: Chiefly from Mauritania
Salt: Saharan salt mines
Iron: Swaziland and Zambia; less frequently from the north
Slaves: From the Sudan to the Islamic countries

RELATIONS BETWEEN AFRICAN REGIONS FROM THE 7TH TO THE 18TH CENTURIES

Illustrations for the earlier period show a man selling blocks of salt, a bracelet, and copper crosses once used as money.

The main event in African history from the 7th to the 11th centuries was the spread of Islam across all of Mediterranean North Africa, from Egypt to Morocco. It is important to note however that the union with the Omayyad Caliphate and the Abbasid Empire in Baghdad lasted only a few centuries and gave way to the development of local North African dynasties—such as the Almoravids—toward the end of the period.

Along the coasts of the Red Sea and the Indian Ocean, the influence of Islam was more direct. Western, central, and eastern Sudan were influenced more indirectly, mainly through trade and culture. The spread of Islam was resisted in certain regions. This occurred chiefly in the Christianized areas of Nubia and Ethiopia, but there was also a strong desire within the Sudanese empires, particularly Ghana, to keep control of the routes to the gold deposits, located near the southern limits of the Sudan. Due to these links between the Islamic world and the Sudan, the immense Sahara Desert became once more a zone of contact between the various peoples living around its edges, just as it had been in

prehistoric times before climatic changes made it a true desert. The use of camels as the primary form of transportation had important influences on every aspect of life in the region. Archeological excavations over recent decades have thoroughly demonstrated the development and variety of cultures present in this area between the 7th and the 11th centuries.

Gold, ivory, and slaves on the one side, and salt on the other, were of fundamental importance to the trade development pattern in Africa. It has been said that African gold in particular determined the spread of Islam across the African continent, although all experts do not agree on this point.

While the spread of Islam played a major role in the development of contacts across the African continent, it is also important to stress that the rest of Africa entered a phase of further development and increased contacts during the same period, and this process did not depend on the influence of Islam. Around the 8th century, most African regions had already entered the Iron Age, and the edges of the tropical forests began to be farmed. The introduction (probably from Madagascar) of

food crops like the banana, the bread tree, and the taro root, which were more suited to the hot humid climates of these regions, was of vital importance to social development. Crops were grown mainly on plantations, with some cereals being cultivated to a lesser degree on the areas of savanna intersecting the forests. With better, more plentiful food, the agricultural communities expanded rapidly. As a result of this increase in numbers, the previous populations of these regions, probably Khoisan (San and Khoikhoi) and Pygmies, were pushed away and became isolated in the desert regions of southern Africa and in small areas of the tropical forests. Tiny groups of these peoples still exist in such areas today.

Around 1100 the basic expansion and shift of the Bantu peoples that had begun at the beginning of the present age drew to a close. Over the centuries, which we could define as the "centuries of formation," the African regions saw a consolidation of certain existing situations and the development of a system of production, particularly for food, that was better organized and more able to satisfy the growing needs of what was probably an ever-increasing population.

Illustrations on this page are representative of cultural changes from the earlier period highlighted on page 60. Africa had entered a period of serious crisis.

Plaque from Benin showing a Portuguese soldier

Portrait of Vasco da Gama on a coin found in Malindi

Swahili merchants

Between 1100 and 1700, North Africa, the Atlantic coastline, and all of the regions along the coast of the Indian Ocean became increasingly important in Africa's relations with other continents. As in the past, relations with the other countries in the Mediterranean basin were continued via the caravan routes across the Sahara Desert and the ports along the North African coast. Relations with Asia were maintained via trade routes across the Indian Ocean. Then from the end of the 15th century, by means of the slave trade, Africa became part of the Atlantic trading system. At least for the coastal regions, this marked the end of Africa's period of isolation.

The inland regions of Africa continued to resist any penetration by outsiders. On the other hand, the relations between the African populations greatly increased and intensified, so much so that at the end of this period no region was left completely isolated from the main trade and cultural networks.

The spread of Islam's influence—religious, cultural, and economic—continued up to the 15th century. We can read proof of this in the writings of many Arab scholars and historians present in Africa over this period. Their writings also mention the decline that began during the 15th century. Trans-Saharan trade continued, but the trade routes gradually shifted toward the east. After the Empire of

Ghana came the Mali and Songhai Empires. The Kanem Bornu Empire rose to importance in the Chad region. Smaller states such as the Hausa city-states and the states between the Upper Niger and the coast came into being due to increasing unrest in the North African regions in and around Morocco.

Trade with the north still involved the same goods: gold, ivory, slaves, and salt. Trade in the south increased. The tropical forests were less of an impassable obstacle than before. The forest margins were burned to make way for agriculture. Some were cleared during the formation of new states along the coasts of the Gulf of Guinea and the Gold Coast. The Atlantic slave trade began in this area and spread down the southern Atlantic coasts, especially to Angola and, to a lesser degree, along the coasts of the Indian Ocean.

Copper and gold remained the basis of trade in East and South Africa. It is important to remember that during this period the Comoros Islands, other smaller archipelagoes, and the great island of Madagascar all became part of the trade network across the Indian Ocean.

At the end of the period between the 12th and 17th centuries, there was a triple fracture in the complicated system of cultural relations and trade networks: 1. The Turkish conquest of a large area of North Africa (Egypt in 1517, Tripoli in 1551, and Tunis in 1574) and the 1591 Moroccan conquest of the Songhai Empire led to serious disruption of the systems of communication across the Sahara. 2. In the east the Portuguese disrupted the Muslim trade routes across the Indian Ocean but failed to gain a solid hold in the region, gradually giving way to other Europeans in the area. 3. Most important was the development of the Atlantic slave trade along the western coasts, which greatly changed the whole picture.

Finally, during the 18th century, Africans lost control of their destiny. They were overwhelmed by European colonial interests and lost their independence for the next 150 years.

Century	West Africa	Central East Africa	South Africa
7th	Arab conquest of North Africa and start of Islamic economic and cultural expansion in the Sudan	The Arabs gain control of the Red Sea; Coptic Christianity takes hold in Nubia and Ethiopia	The expansion of the Bantu peoples continues as does the Indonesian colonization of Madagascar begun in the first centuries A.D.
8th	Development of trans-Saharan trade		
9th		Birth of the Kingdom of Kanem	Probable beginning of the Great Zimbabwe
9th–11th	Empire of Ghana	Trade networks in the Indian Ocean become more complex	
12th–14th	Empire of Mali	Islamic influence on Kanem, which becomes Kanem Bornu	Gold exported to India
15th	Songhai Empire; Portugal begins voyages of discovery via Africa to India; expeditions of Dias and Vasco da Gama	Development of Swahili civilizations	Height of splendor in reign of Monomotapa Zimbabwe
16th	Start of Atlantic slave trade; Portuguese relations with Benin and Congo	Portuguese arrive in Indian Ocean	Struggles between Madagascan kingdoms
17th	European forts built on Gold Coast	Decline of Islamic supremacy in Indian Ocean and decline of Kingdom of Ethiopia	Height of reign of Imerina in Madagascar; Dutch found Fort Cape, nucleus of future Cape Colony
18th	Height of Atlantic slave trade	French and English take over from Portuguese in Indian Ocean	

Sculpture from Mopti or Jenne, Kingdom of Mali (16th century A.D.) The Dogon figure is that of an ancestor.

CHRONOLOGY

Bantu sculpture (in the Musee de l'Homme in Paris)

Axe shaft in hard-wood, from Malawi or Mozambique

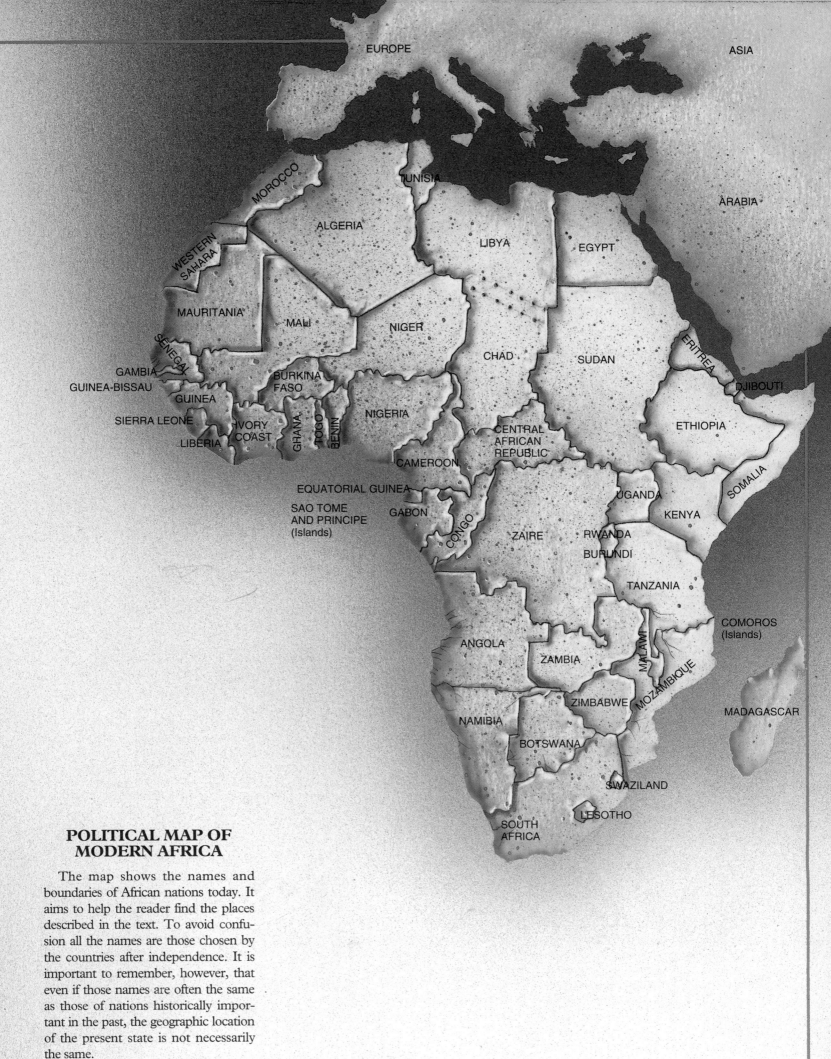

EUROPE

ASIA

ARABIA

MOROCCO

TUNISIA

ALGERIA

LIBYA

EGYPT

WESTERN
SAHARA

MAURITANIA

MALI

NIGER

CHAD

SUDAN

ERITREA

SENEGAL

GAMBIA

GUINEA-BISSAU

GUINEA

DJIBOUTI

BURKINA
FASO

SIERRA LEONE

LIBERIA

IVORY
COAST

GHANA

TOGO

BENIN

NIGERIA

ETHIOPIA

CENTRAL
AFRICAN
REPUBLIC

CAMEROON

SOMALIA

EQUATORIAL GUINEA

UGANDA

SAO TOME
AND PRINCIPE
(Islands)

GABON

CONGO

ZAIRE

RWANDA

BURUNDI

KENYA

TANZANIA

ANGOLA

ZAMBIA

MALAWI

MOZAMBIQUE

COMOROS
(Islands)

MADAGASCAR

ZIMBABWE

NAMIBIA

BOTSWANA

SWAZILAND

LESOTHO

SOUTH
AFRICA

POLITICAL MAP OF
MODERN AFRICA

The map shows the names and
boundaries of African nations today. It
aims to help the reader find the places
described in the text. To avoid confusion all the names are those chosen by
the countries after independence. It is
important to remember, however, that
even if those names are often the same
as those of nations historically important in the past, the geographic location
of the present state is not necessarily
the same.

GLOSSARY

Afro-Asiatic languages: Linguistic group occupying upper third of Africa from the Indian Ocean to the Atlantic Ocean, except for area of Nilo-Saharan languages

Allah: The one true God of the Muslim faith

Amharic: Language of the people of Ethiopia

animist: Worshipper of inanimate objects or objects in nature

anthropology: The study of human beings in relation to distribution origin, physical character, and culture

archeological digs: The exploration site of archeologists

archeology: Scientific study of remains of past human life and activities

archipelago: Expanse of water with many scattered islands

ardin: Stringed musical instrument of Africa

asantehene: Word for "king" used by Ashanti people

Bantu: Term used by linguistic scholars to show linkage among languages in sub-Saharan Africa; a member of any group of Africans who speak a Bantu language.

basin: Topographic area about a lake or river that collects water

bifacial tools: Two-faced implements with opposite cutting or scraping edges

Bronze Age: Period of human culture characterized by the use of bronze that began between 4000 and 3000 BC

Byzantines: Members of the Byzantine Empire of the fifth and sixth centuries

caliph: A successor of Mohammed as temporal and religious head of the Islamic faith

caravan: Group of people who travel together for protection through arid or hostile lands

caravel: Large sailing ship of fifteenth and sixteenth centuries

carnivore: Flesh-eating animal

cassava: Plant with fleshy edible rootstock grown in the tropics

commodity: An economic good or article of commerce, unfortunately embracing humans in the slave trade

Congo: Area in central Africa that was the site of ancient kingdoms, and now nation of Zaire; a principal Bantu language

Coptic Christians: Members of a traditional Christian church originating in Egypt who believe in the divine nature of Christ, but not in the idea of his human form

cowry shells: At one time official money in the Congo

depression: An area of lower altitude than the surrounding area, a depression tends to collect water forming lakes and rivers

desertification: Process of becoming arid land or desert because of land mismanagement or climate change

digging stick: Primitive tool to make holes to plant seeds in early period of agriculture

dugout canoe: Boat made by hollowing out a log

dynasty: Succession of rulers of the same line of descent

emigration, forced: Departure from one's country against one's will

Ethiopia: Ancient country of northeast Africa, now site of an independent state

ethnobotany: Study of the food crops produced by people of different world regions

ethnology: Study of different world cultures

farba (also farin): Administrative official who governed the commoners and was appointed by the Mali king

fetish: Object believed among primitive people to have magical power

feudal federation: Organization of different peoples, tribes, or small kingdoms that pay homage, taxes, and in general are subordinate to another, more powerful state

figurative arts: Representations of form or figure in arts, such as sculpture

fossil: Remnant or trace of an animal or plant of past geologic ages

Ge'ez: Language once spoken in Ethiopia and still used in Orthodox Ethiopian churches

ghirbe: Goatskin container used for carrying water

Gold Coast: European name for the coastal region of West Africa, center for the gold trade; coast of the Gulf of Guinea

granary: Storehouse for threshed grain

"Great Shelter": Council chamber of a Dogon village

griots: Oral historians and musicians of western African societies

habitat: Place or type of site where a plant or animal normally lives and grows

Hausa: Language of the Hausa people, used as a trade language between local people and outside merchants; also early city-state in what is present-day Nigeria. *See Swahili*

"holy wars" (jihad): Islamic movement to establish or reestablish the "true" faith in a region

Homo sapiens: Man, human species of the genus of primate mammals

Hypotheses: Tentative assumptions made to test their logical consequences

invertebrate: Animal that lacks a spinal column

Iron Age: Period of human culture characterized by the use of iron, beginning somewhat before 1000 BC

Islam: Monotheistic religious faith of Muslims

Ivory Coast: European name for the area of the coastal region of West Africa that was once the center for the ivory trade

khamsa: Name given to the hand in North Africa, which represents the five fundamental principles of Islam

Khoisan languages: Linguistic group occupying roughly Angola and Namibia

Koran: Muslim book of sacred writings

lemur: Nocturnal mammal now found almost exclusively in Madagascar

linguistics: Study of the characteristics of languages

lost wax method: Process of metal casting in which a model of wax is made, coated with a heat resistant material to form a mold of an object, the wax is then melted away and molten metal is poured into the mold

Luba: Bantu language spoken in Zaire

Malagasy dialects: Linguistic group occupying Madagascar

mani: Regional rulers in the Congo under the manikongo

manikongo: Name used for "king" in Congo

mansa: African term signifying "king"

maquis: Region of dense growth of small trees and bushes on Mediterranean shore

matrilineage: The system of tracing descent through mother's family

medicine man: Priestly healer or sorcerer supposedly with magical powers

Mesolithic Age: Period of the Stone Age between the Paleolithic and Neolithic Ages

Miji kenda: Bantu language spoken in coastal Kenya

millet: Small seed cereal or forage grass

Mohammed: Allah's prophet according to the religious faith of Muslims

monarchy: Nation or state having one sovereign ruler

Monophysite: Form of Christianity that holds Christ's nature was exclusively divine

monsoon: Periodic wind in the Indian Ocean and southern Asia

negus: Ethiopian word for "ruler"

Niger-Congo languages: Linguistic group occupying middle third of Africa from the western lands drained by the Senegal and Niger Rivers, across Equatorial Africa south of Lake Victoria to the Indian Ocean, except for the area of Khoisan languages

Nilo-Saharan languages: Linguistic group occupying section of the Upper Nile River, southern Sudan, Chad, eastern Niger, and the Niger River north of Kainji Lake

nkoni: Three-stringed guitar

nomad: Member of a wandering pastoral people

oni: Name given to Ifi king

oral tradition: Practice of handing down information, customs, and beliefs by word of mouth

Paleolithic Age: Second period of the Stone Age characterized by use of chipped stone implements

patriarchal society: One that traces descent through father's family

pharoah: Ruler of ancient Egypt

pidgin language: Simplified speech used between people with different native languages

pilgrimage: Journey of a believer to a shrine or sacred place

plantation: Large, self-sustaining agricultural estate usually planted to a single crop, where owners, administrators, and workers live, and which at one time may have been worked by slave labor

polygamy: Practice in marriage of having more than one spouse at the same time

pombeiros: Slaves who manned caravans for the Portugese

prehistoric times: Period that antedates written history

Proto-Bantu: That group of Bantu speakers who are the origin of all Bantu speakers

raffia: The fiber of the raffia palm tree, woven to produce mats that were sometimes used as money in Luango, Africa

rain forest: Tropical woodland with an annual rainfall of at least 100 inches and marked by lofty broad-leaved evergreen trees forming a continuous canopy

ras: Ethiopian word for "provincial ruler"

Sahara: Arabic for "empty," as used in Sahara Desert

Sahel: Semiarid bushland south of the Sahara Desert

savanna: Tropical or subtropical grassland containing scattered trees and drought-resistant undergrowth

sharif: One of noble ancestry or political preeminence in Islamic countries

Shona: Bantu language spoken in Zimbabwe

"silent trade": Term used to describe how Europeans put out goods for trade with African who put their goods opposite, both adding and subtracting as they believed an equal or fair trade could be reached

Slave Coast: European name for the coastal region of West Africa, center of the slave trade

smelting: Process of melting or fusing ore to separate the metal

souk: Marketplace in northern Africa

Stone Age: First period known of prehistoric human culture characterized by the use of stone tools

sub-Saharan Africa: Those regions of the African continent lying immediately south of the Sahara Desert

Sudan: Name of Arabic origin, meaning "land of the black men"; refers to savanna area between the Sahara Desert and the tropical forest

surplus foodstuffs: Food supplies, grown or manufactured, that are more than sufficient for the producer's use and thereby sold or traded

Swahili: Language formed from mergers of trading cultures and widely spoken in Africa

syncretism: Combination of different forms of religious beliefs or practices

taro root: Tropical plant with edible tuberous rootstock

terra-cotta: Glazed or unglazed fired brownish-orange clay used for statuettes and vases, roofing, and ornamentation

trade fairs: In Africa, trade activities between people from the interior and Indian Ocean traders during southerly monsoon seasons

tributes: Taxes paid by a people or vassal state to another state for protection or for trade or passage privileges

tubule: Reedlike musical instrument native to Africa

ulemas: Important experts on the Muslim faith

vassal state: A state that is dependent on another state for protection and general economic well-being

Windward Coast: European name for the coastal region of West Africa, where trade winds (prevailing winds) made navigation difficult

worudwad: Shield made from animal skin and used by Tuareg warriors

Xhosa: Bantu language spoken in South Africa

INDEX

collapse of, 30
as confederation, 28
court of, 28
extent of, 26
as feudal federation, 25
justice in, 27, 29
map, before and after Sundiata, 26
mineral wealth of, 29
rise of, 23
after Sundiata, 26-27
and Sundiata, 24-25
See also Mande civilization
Malinke kingdom, 24
Mamluk knight, *17*
Mamluk territory, *17*
Mande civilization, 28-29
expansion of, 22
griots of, 11
map of ancient kingdom of, *23*
See also Ghana Empire; Mali Empire; Old
Manding
mani, 48
manikongo, 48, 50
mansa, 28
Mansa Musa, 26, 30
maquis, Mediterranean, *5*
Marinid, sultan of Morocco, 31
marketplace, Congo, *52-53*
Masudi, Al-, 9
matrilineage, 21
Mauretania, 20
Mbundu people, 47
Mecca, 16, 26
medicine men, 11
Mediterranean coastal strip, 8, *9*
Mediterranean Sea trade, 45
Merina kingdom, 43
Meroe, 36
Mesolithic Age, *6*, 7
Middle Ages, 18
middlemen, slave trade, 17
Miji Kenda language, 14
milk pail, *25*
millet, *10*
Mogadishu, 38, 40
Mohammed, 16
Mombasa, 40
Monomotapa kingdom, 54, 55
Monophysite Christianity, 36
monotheism, 16
monsoon winds, 38, 40
Morocco, 17, 30, 31

and conquest of Songhai Empire, 61
decline of, 26
unrest in, 61
Mosque of Tinmallal, *17*
Mossi people, 30, 31, 35
musical instruments
in Mali Empire, 29
in Mande culture, *28, 29*
nkoni, 11
in Uganda, *10*
Muslim city, market scene in, *39*
Muslim dynasties in Africa, 16
See also Islam
Muslim warrior, 35

N

Narin Famakhan, 24-25
Ndongo people, 47
Niani, 25, 26
Niger-Congo languages, *4*, 7, 34
Nigerian region, 34-35
Nigerian woman, *27*
Niger River, 20, 30, 31
mouth of, *14*
Nile cataracts, 36
Nile Valley, 8, *9*, 12
Nilo-Saharan languages, *4*
Nilo-Saharan peoples, 14
nkoni (musical instrument), 11
Nok civilization, 6
Nok culture, 34
nomads, 12, 20, 33
Nopata, 36
North and South America, (map) *56-57*
Nubia, 8, *9*, 36-37
repulsion of Arabs by, 16-17
resistance of, to Islam, 60
treaty with Arabs, 36

O

oases, 12
Old Manding, 23
Omayyad Caliphate, 60
Omayyad dynasty, *16*
Opuku Ware, 35
oral tradition, 10-11, 18, 24-25, 30, 35, 46, 55
limitations of, 21
problems of, 11
Oromo Galla people, 37
Orthodox Ethiopian Church, 37
Osei Tutu, 35

Ottoman territory, *17*
Ouagadougou, 31
Ovambo people, 47, 49
overland trade routes, 38
Ovimbundo people, 47, 49

P

Paleolithic Age, 6, 7
patriarchal society, 15
"Periplus of the Erythraen Sea, The," 38
Peul. See Fulani people
pharoah, 50
Phoenician civilization, 7
Phoenician ships, 19
pidgin language, 53
pile-dwelling, *9*
pilgrimage(s)
of Askia Mohammed, 30-31
of Mansa Musa, 26
plantations, 60
polygamy, 28
pombeiros, 53
Portuguese
accounts of Benin, 35
on coast of West Africa, 19
in the Congo, 47
and gold trade, 40
interest of, in Ethiopia, 37
missionary activity of, 45, 48-49, 55
in southern Africa, 55
vs. Spanish in New World, 56-57
and Swahili, 40-41
voyages of discovery, 45
prehistoric ages in Africa, (graph) *6*
prehistoric cultures in Africa, *6*
prehistoric tools, 7
Proto-Bantu, 7
expansion, *6*
language tree, *9*
Ptolemy, Claudius, 38
Pygmies, *9*, 60

R

race, defined, 4
raffia
as currency, 52
mats, *51, 52*, 53
rain forest, 8
Ras of Shoa, 37
Red Sea coast, 38
religion